Hedge Funds, Leverage, and the Lessons of Long-Term Capital Management

Report of
The President's Working Group on Financial Markets

Department of the Treasury	Board of Governors of the Federal Reserve System	Securities and Exchange Commission	Commodity Futures Trading Commission

April 1999

April 28, 1999

The Honorable J. Dennis Hastert
The Speaker
United States House of Representatives
Washington, D.C. 20515

Dear Mr. Speaker:

We are pleased to transmit the report of the President's Working Group on Financial Markets on Hedge Funds, Leverage, and the Lessons of Long-Term Capital Management (LTCM).

The principal policy issue arising out of the events surrounding the near collapse of LTCM is how to constrain excessive leverage. By increasing the chance that problems at one financial institution could be transmitted to other institutions, excessive leverage can increase the likelihood of a general breakdown in the functioning of financial markets. This issue is not limited to hedge funds; other financial institutions are often larger and more highly leveraged than most hedge funds.

In view of our findings, the Working Group recommends a number of measures designed to constrain excessive leverage. These measures are designed to improve transparency in the system, enhance private sector risk management practices, develop more risk-sensitive approaches to capital adequacy, support financial contract netting in the event of bankruptcy, and encourage offshore financial centers to comply with international standards.

The LTCM incident highlights a number of tax issues with respect to hedge funds, including the tax treatment of total return equity swaps and the use of offshore financial centers. These issues, however, are beyond the scope of this report and are being addressed separately by Treasury.

A number of other federal agencies were full participants in this study and support its conclusions and recommendations: the Council of Economic Advisers, the Federal Deposit Insurance Corporation, the National Economic Council, the Federal Reserve Bank of New York, the Office of the Comptroller of the Currency, and the Office of Thrift Supervision. We are grateful for their extensive assistance.

We appreciate the opportunity to convey this report to you, and we look forward to continuing to work with you on these important issues.

Sincerely,

(signed)   (signed)
Robert E. Rubin   Alan Greenspan
Secretary   Chairman
Department of the Treasury   Board of Governors of the Federal Reserve

(signed)   (signed)
Arthur Levitt   Brooksley Born
Chairman   Chairperson
Securities and Exchange Commission   Commodity Futures Trading Commission

April 28, 1999

The Honorable Al Gore
President of the Senate
United States Senate
Washington, D.C. 20510

Dear Mr. President:

We are pleased to transmit the report of the President's Working Group on Financial Markets on Hedge Funds, Leverage, and the Lessons of Long-Term Capital Management (LTCM).

The principal policy issue arising out of the events surrounding the near collapse of LTCM is how to constrain excessive leverage. By increasing the chance that problems at one financial institution could be transmitted to other institutions, excessive leverage can increase the likelihood of a general breakdown in the functioning of financial markets. This issue is not limited to hedge funds; other financial institutions are often larger and more highly leveraged than most hedge funds.

In view of our findings, the Working Group recommends a number of measures designed to constrain excessive leverage. These measures are designed to improve transparency in the system, enhance private sector risk management practices, develop more risk-sensitive approaches to capital adequacy, support financial contract netting in the event of bankruptcy, and encourage offshore financial centers to comply with international standards.

The LTCM incident highlights a number of tax issues with respect to hedge funds, including the tax treatment of total return equity swaps and the use of offshore financial centers. These issues, however, are beyond the scope of this report and are being addressed separately by Treasury.

A number of other federal agencies were full participants in this study and support its conclusions and recommendations: the Council of Economic Advisers, the Federal Deposit Insurance Corporation, the National Economic Council, the Federal Reserve Bank of New York, the Office of the Comptroller of the Currency, and the Office of Thrift Supervision. We are grateful for their extensive assistance.

We appreciate the opportunity to convey this report to you, and we look forward to continuing to work with you on these important issues.

Sincerely,

(signed)
Robert E. Rubin
Secretary
Department of the Treasury

(signed)
Alan Greenspan
Chairman
Board of Governors of the Federal Reserve

(signed)
Arthur Levitt
Chairman
Securities and Exchange Commission

(signed)
Brooksley Born
Chairperson
Commodity Futures Trading Commission

TABLE OF CONTENTS

Page

EXECUTIVE SUMMARY

The President's Working Group on Financial Markets recommends a number of measures designed to constrain excessive leverage in the financial system. The events in global financial markets in the summer and fall of 1998 demonstrated that excessive leverage can greatly magnify the negative effects of any event or series of events on the financial system as a whole. The near collapse of Long-Term Capital Management ("LTCM"), a private sector investment firm, highlighted the possibility that problems at one financial institution could be transmitted to other institutions, and potentially pose risks to the financial system.

Although LTCM is a hedge fund, this issue is not limited to hedge funds. Other financial institutions, including some banks and securities firms, are larger, and generally more highly leveraged, than hedge funds.

While leverage can play a positive role in our financial system, problems can arise when financial institutions go too far in extending credit to their customers and counterparties. The near collapse of LTCM illustrates the need for all participants in our financial system, not only hedge funds, to face constraints on the amount of leverage they assume.

Our market-based economy relies primarily on market discipline to constrain leverage. But market discipline can break down. In the case of LTCM, its investors, creditors, and counterparties did not provide an effective check on its overall activities. Moreover, some of the same market and credit risk management weaknesses that permitted LTCM to achieve its extraordinary leverage were evident in other market participants. In the immediate aftermath of LTCM's near collapse, credit risk management practices vis-a-vis highly leveraged institutions were tightened. But market history indicates that even painful lessons recede from memory with time.

Therefore, the Working Group recommends the following measures:

- More frequent and meaningful information on hedge funds should be made public.

- Public companies, including financial institutions, should publicly disclose additional information about their material financial exposures to significantly leveraged institutions, including hedge funds.

- Financial institutions should enhance their practices for counterparty risk management.

- Regulators should encourage improvements in the risk-management systems of regulated entities.

- Regulators should promote the development of more risk-sensitive but prudent approaches to capital adequacy.

- Regulators need expanded risk assessment authority for the unregulated affiliates of broker-dealers and futures commission merchants.[*]

- The Congress should enact the provisions proposed by the President's Working Group to support financial contract netting.

- Regulators should consider stronger incentives to encourage offshore financial centers to comply with international standards.

The Working Group will be monitoring and assessing the effectiveness of the measures outlined above. If further evidence emerges that indirect regulation of currently unregulated market participants is not effective in constraining excessive leverage, there are several matters that could be given further consideration; however, the Working Group is not recommending any of them at this time.

Concerns have been expressed about the activities of highly leveraged institutions with respect to their impact on market dynamics generally and vulnerable economies in particular. Such activity can affect markets in some circumstances and for limited periods although, as a number of independent studies that have been undertaken so far have suggested, the activities of highly leveraged institutions do not appear to have played a significant role in precipitating the financial market crises of the past few years. Further study of this issue will be undertaken by the Financial Stability Forum, recently established by the G-7.

This report includes a Background section that provides a description of hedge funds, their activities and their counterparties, and also describes the events surrounding the near collapse of LTCM. The second section, on Public Policy Issues, discusses a number of questions raised by LTCM. In the Conclusions and Recommendations section we fully discuss the recommendations summarized above. This report also includes a number of appendices that address some key topics in more detail.

---

[*] Please see footnote 23 on page 39.

Hedge Funds, Leverage, and the Lessons of Long-Term Capital Management

Report of
The President's Working Group on Financial Markets

I. BACKGROUND

HEDGE FUNDS [1]

A. General Description

The term "hedge fund" is commonly used to describe a variety of different types of investment vehicles that share some similar characteristics. Although it is not statutorily defined, the term encompasses any pooled investment vehicle that is privately organized, administered by professional investment managers, and not widely available to the public. The primary investors in hedge funds are wealthy individuals and institutional investors. In addition, hedge fund managers frequently have a stake in the funds they manage. Entities classified as hedge funds are commonly organized as limited partnerships or limited liability companies, and in many cases are domiciled outside the United States.

Hedge funds are not a recent invention, as the founding of the first hedge fund is conventionally dated to 1949.[2] A 1968 survey by the Securities and Exchange Commission ("SEC") identified 140 funds operating at that time. During the last two decades, however, the hedge fund industry has grown substantially. Although it is difficult to estimate precisely the size of the industry, a number of estimates indicate that as of mid-1998 there were between 2,500 and 3,500 hedge funds managing between $200 billion and $300 billion in capital, with approximately $800 billion to $1 trillion in total assets. Collectively, hedge funds remain relatively small when compared to other sectors of the U.S. financial markets. At the end of 1998, for instance, commercial banks had $4.1 trillion in total assets; mutual funds had assets of approximately $5

---

[1] This section provides a summary of the key background information on hedge funds. Additional information about hedge funds is presented in Appendix A of this report.

[2] For a detailed history of hedge funds, see Ted Caldwell, "Introduction: The Model for Superior Performance," in *Hedge Funds: Investment and Portfolio Strategies for the Institutional Investor*, eds. Jess Lederman and Robert A. Klein (New York: Irwin Professional Publishing, 1995), pp. 1-17.

trillion; private pension funds had $4.3 trillion; state and local retirement funds had $2.3 trillion; and insurance companies had assets of $3.7 trillion.[3]

With $200 - $300 billion spread among approximately 3,000 hedge funds, most hedge funds are relatively small, with the vast majority controlling less than $100 million in invested capital. In fact, according to commodity pool operator ("CPO") filings with the CFTC, there are perhaps only a few dozen hedge funds today that have a capital base larger than $1 billion, and only a small handful that exceed $5 billion.[4] The very largest hedge funds have less than $12 billion in investor capital, although some "families" of funds have greater stakes. Although individually and as an industry, hedge funds represent a relatively small segment of the market, their impact is greatly magnified by their highly active trading strategies and by the leverage obtained through their use of repurchase agreements and derivative contracts.

Apart from size, hedge funds differ in other important ways from alternative types of investment vehicles. Hedge funds are able to sell securities short and to buy securities on leverage. While this activity is not unique to hedge funds, hedge funds often use leverage aggressively. Hedge funds also charge advisory fees based on performance, and they tend to pursue short-term investment strategies.

In general, active market participants such as hedge funds can provide benefits to financial markets by enhancing liquidity and efficiency. Additionally, they can play a role in financial innovation and the reallocation of financial risk. However, some hedge funds, like other large highly leveraged financial institutions, also have the potential to disrupt the functioning of financial markets. Indeed, some observers have asserted that hedge funds are responsible for large and sometimes disruptive market movements in vulnerable economies. According to several comprehensive analyses of the issue, however, hedge funds do not appear to have played a significant role in precipitating the financial market crises of the past few years.[5] Further study of this issue will be undertaken by the Financial Stability Forum, recently established by the G-7.

There is no single market strategy or approach pursued by hedge funds as a group. Rather, hedge funds exhibit a wide variety of investment styles, some of which use highly

---

[3] Source: Board of Governors of the Federal Reserve System, *Flow of Funds Accounts of the United States*, Fourth Quarter 1998.

[4] The CFTC has limited regulatory authority over CPOs, including those CPOs that operate hedge funds, that either transact business on U.S. futures exchanges or that have U.S. investors and transact business on U.S. or foreign futures exchanges. It should be further noted that not all hedge funds are operated by persons required to register as CPOs. For more information on CPOs, see Appendix C.

[5] See Barry Eichengreen et al., *Hedge Funds and Financial Market Dynamics*, Occasional Paper No. 166 (Washington D.C.: International Monetary Fund, 1998); and Stephen J. Brown, William N. Goetzmann, and James M. Park, *Hedge Funds and the Asian Currency Crisis of 1997*, NBER Working Paper No. 6427 (February 1998).

quantitative techniques while others employ more subjective factors. Researchers and other industry observers therefore often classify hedge funds according to the main investment strategy practiced by the funds' management. Global-macro funds, for instance, take positions based on their forecasts of global macroeconomic developments, while event-driven funds invest in specific securities related to such events as bankruptcies, reorganizations, and mergers. A relatively small set of market-neutral hedge funds employ relative-value strategies seeking to profit by taking offsetting positions in two assets whose price relationships are expected to move in a direction favorable to these offsetting positions.

Hedge funds are also diverse in their use of different types of financial instruments. Many hedge funds trade equity or fixed income securities, taking either long or short positions, or sometimes both simultaneously. A large number of funds also use exchange-traded futures contracts or over-the-counter ("OTC") derivatives, to hedge their portfolios, to exploit market inefficiencies, or to take outright positions. Still others are active participants in foreign exchange markets. In general, hedge funds are more active users of derivatives and of short positions than are mutual funds or many other classes of asset managers. In this respect, the trading activities of hedge funds are similar to those undertaken by the proprietary trading areas of large commercial and investment banks.

Hedge funds that conform to certain requirements are eligible for various exemptions from federal securities laws. In particular, unlike mutual funds, hedge funds are exempt from SEC reporting requirements, as well as from regulatory restrictions on leverage or trading strategies. They also face fewer limitations on the structure and size of fees they may charge. The sponsors of hedge funds that trade on organized futures exchanges and that have U.S. investors, however, are typically required to register with the CFTC as a CPO. Registered CPOs are subject to periodic reporting, recordkeeping, and disclosure requirements.

To avoid the registration and reporting requirements of the federal securities laws, hedge funds generally do not raise funds via public offerings of their securities, advertise broadly, or engage in general solicitation. Hedge funds also typically have either no more than 100 beneficial owners or require their investors to meet rigid minimum size requirements.[6]

Recent studies of hedge fund performance have generally found that hedge funds as a group offer greater return, yet greater risk, than investment benchmarks such as Standard and Poor's S&P 500 stock index.[7] Not surprisingly, particular classes of hedge funds have at times

---

[6] Sections 3(c)(1) — limiting beneficial ownership to 100 persons — and 3(c)(7) — limiting investment to "qualified purchasers" — of the Investment Company Act of 1940. For a detailed discussion of these provisions, see Appendix B of this report.

[7] See, for example, William Fung and David Hsieh, "Empirical Characteristics of Dynamic Trading Strategies: The Case of Hedge Funds." *Review of Financial Studies* 10:2 (Summer 1997) pp. 275 - 302; and Stephen J. Brown, William N. Goetzmann, and Roger G. Ibbotson, "Off-Shore Hedge Funds: Survival and Performance 1989 - 1995." *Journal of Business* 72:1 (January 1999) pp. 91-117.

outperformed benchmark measures on a risk-adjusted basis, while other classes have at times underperformed. Importantly, the performance of many hedge funds historically has not been highly correlated with overall market performance, thus accounting for their inclusion in the portfolios of wealthy individuals and institutional investors who seek a broad diversification of their investments.

B. Trading Practices

Hedge funds are only one example of a collection of institutions that actively trade securities and derivative instruments. An assessment of the public policy issues posed by hedge funds might therefore benefit from a consideration of hedge funds in the broader context of trading activity. In today's economy, the markets for traded securities are performing an increasingly important role in the intermediation of credit. Among the wide range of institutions participating in this trading activity are hedge funds, trading desks of banks, securities firms and insurance companies, mutual funds, and other managed funds. Some of these institutions engage in trading activity more intensively than others.

The diverse collection of institutions, including hedge funds, that engage in trading activity can be characterized by similarities in their use of mark-to-market discipline, leverage, and active trading.

Mark-to-market

Mark-to-market practices, the discipline of periodically valuing positions at current market prices, may be imposed through external accounting or regulatory requirements, or through internal risk management practices. In addition, mark-to-market practices may be imposed through counterparties' valuation of trading exposures and collateral. This discipline is useful for preventing the concealment of losses and for encouraging the timely resolution of problems. While they may not necessarily be required to do so, hedge funds generally practice this discipline.

The use of mark-to-market valuation for managing collateral and variation margin to mitigate credit risk can impose cash flow and liquidity strains on a trading entity. Such liquidity and cash flow problems can be particularly severe for a highly leveraged trading vehicle, especially during episodes of extreme price volatility when mark-to-market driven collateral and margin calls can impose a very short time frame for resolving liquidity problems.

Leverage

Leverage allows hedge funds to magnify their exposures and, as a direct consequence, magnify their risks. The term leverage can be defined in balance-sheet terms, in which case it refers to the ratio of assets to net worth. Alternatively, leverage can be defined in terms of risk, in which case it is a measure of economic risk relative to capital. Hedge funds obtain economic leverage in various ways, such as through the use of repurchase agreements, short positions, and derivative contracts. At times, the choice of investment is influenced by the availability of leverage. Beyond a trading institution's risk appetite, both balance-sheet and economic leverage may be constrained in some cases by initial margin and collateral at the transaction level, and also by trading and credit limits imposed by trading counterparties. For some types of financial institutions, regulatory capital requirements may constrain leverage, although this limitation does not apply to hedge funds. Hedge funds are limited in their use of leverage only by the willingness of their creditors and counterparties to provide such leverage.

Hedge funds vary greatly in their use of leverage. Nevertheless, compared with other trading institutions, hedge funds' use of leverage, combined with any structured or illiquid positions whose full value cannot be realized in a quick sale, can potentially make them somewhat fragile institutions that are vulnerable to liquidity shocks. While trading desks of banks and securities firms may take positions similar to hedge funds' investments, these organizations and their parent firms often have both liquidity sources and independent streams of income from other activities that can offset the riskiness of their positions.

Like banks and securities firms, but unlike most mutual funds, hedge funds lever their capital bases to increase their total asset holdings by a multiple of the amount of capital invested in the funds. CPO reports, however, suggest that the significant majority of reporting hedge funds have balance-sheet leverage ratios (total assets to capital) of less than 2-to-1. There are, of course, important exceptions. According to September 1998 CPO filings, at least ten hedge funds with capital exceeding $100 million leveraged their capital more than ten times. At the extreme, the most leveraged hedge funds in this group levered their capital more than thirty times.

Active trading

Active trading, which is typical of hedge funds, is a practice in which investment positions are changed with high frequency. Such trading may be conducted to maintain a desired risk-return profile as market prices fluctuate, or it may be conducted to attempt to profit from short-term changes in prices. While turnover in hedge funds' portfolios differs widely, the typical hedge fund's use of active trading strategies is closer to that of financial intermediaries' proprietary trading desks than to a mutual fund or pension fund.

Active trading strategies rely on market liquidity and access to credit to meet funding needs. However, an entity's ability to trade actively can diminish either because creditworthiness concerns cause counterparties to cut trading and credit limits or because of a broader disappearance of market liquidity. The inability to execute active trading strategies can lead to unexpectedly large mark-to-market losses as positions that had been thought of as modifiable exposures become longer-term positions.

C. Disclosure and Monitoring

A trading entity is often subject to disclosure and monitoring of its financial condition, and these requirements can serve to limit the trader's activities. Trading desks of a few major banks and securities firms are constrained by internal risk management functions, by risk-based capital requirements,[8] and by public disclosure of the firms' overall trading activity.[9] No such limitations apply, however, to hedge funds. In fact, hedge funds are subject to fewer public disclosure requirements and less monitoring than many other financial institutions.

Disclosures by hedge funds to counterparties and investors are often made using accounting and balance-sheet concepts. While such information includes notional amount and market value of derivatives contracts, the typical accounting statement is still not informative about the risk profile of trading activity (*e.g.*, the nature of the exposures to market risk and credit risk).

D. Counterparty and Credit Relationships

In order for hedge funds to conduct their active trading and to employ leverage, it is necessary for them to enter into business relationships with other entities. This section describes the nature of these relationships.

Credit exposures

Credit exposures between hedge funds and their counterparties arise primarily from trading and lending relationships, such as through derivatives and repurchase agreement ("repo") transactions.[10] These exposures, which are often reciprocal, are created when changes in market prices cause the replacement values of transactions to rise above their value at inception. Thus, a default of either the hedge fund or the counterparty would cause a loss to the other party because the transactions can only be replaced at the market prices prevailing after default.

---

[8] Banks' trading activity is subject to risk-based regulatory capital requirements. Securities firms are also subject to regulatory capital requirements.

[9] For example, some banks disclose both the prospective and retrospective volatility of their trading revenues in the form of both value-at risk ("VaR") and the realized variability of trading revenues.

[10] A repurchase agreement ("repo") is the sale of a security, often – though not always – a U.S. government obligation or other highly liquid instrument, at a specified price coupled with a simultaneous agreement to buy back the security on a specified future date, usually at a fixed or determinable price. A reverse repurchase agreement is the purchase of a security with an agreement to sell it back. Thus, from the perspective of one party these coupled transactions constitute a repo and to the other party, a reverse repo. Interest normally flows to the provider of funds (the party doing the reverse repo) from the provider of securities (the party doing the repo).

The credit exposure of a typical transaction has two components, the current credit exposure and the potential future exposure. The current credit exposure at a moment in time is the market value of the contract, and represents the replacement cost of the contract if one party to the transaction defaults at that moment. The potential future exposure is an estimate of the possible increase in the contract's replacement value from the point of view of a particular firm over a specified interval in the future, such as between the time of a potential default and the time the counterparty is able to replace the contract.

In addition to the credit exposures stemming from trading relationships, further credit exposure may be realized by counterparties when they extend credit to hedge funds through credit lines. Hedge funds can face considerable liquidity risk through mismatched cash flows of assets and liabilities. Revolving lines of credit and broker loans are sometimes used to bridge these mismatches. However, these credit lines often entail high costs, and thus are not typically used for establishing leverage. Hedge funds can achieve economic leverage in their positions more cheaply in other ways, such as through repo and derivatives transactions.

Counterparties manage these exposures through a variety of safeguards including due diligence, disclosure, collateral practices, credit limits, and monitoring.

Due diligence and documentation

Due diligence reviews by extenders of credit to hedge fund customers typically include assessments of: offering circulars or private placement memorandums; partnership agreements; performance history; investment authority; management ability and reputation; capital, including size, growth, investor concentration, and management share of the capital base; risk profile implications of the fund's investment and trading styles; liquidity, including types of positions and investor withdrawal rules; leverage, including on- and off-balance-sheet leverage, and fit with liquidity of positions; risk management; and front and back office operations.

In addition to such reviews, maintaining up-to-date documentation of all outstanding contracts is an important component of credit-risk management. Generally, signed master agreements are required prior to initiation of transactions. In cases where a continuing business relationship has not been established and master agreements have not been signed, "full" confirmations containing many of the provisions found in a master agreement are used. Master agreements usually include standard ISDA (International Swaps and Derivatives Association) and IFEMA (International Foreign Exchange Master Agreement) default clauses, supplemented with additional termination events covering the dissolution or liquidation of the fund, the resignation of the fund's general partner or principals, or decreases in net asset values beyond a certain threshold.

Information provided to counterparties

Banks and securities firms typically impose on-going financial reporting requirements on their hedge fund customers as part of their credit-risk assessment and risk-management process. Such reporting usually includes audited annual financial statements, quarterly financial statements, and monthly net asset value statements.

The variability of a hedge fund's financial position and risk profile, however, makes traditional tools of financial statement analysis less effective in assessing the credit exposure to a hedge fund. As noted in a 1994 Bank for International Settlements ("BIS") report on public disclosure of risks arising from trading activity, traditional accounting-based information is not alone sufficient to describe the risks associated with trading activity.[11] That report emphasized the importance of information about the volatility of trading portfolio values, both retrospectively and prospectively, for assessing a counterparty's creditworthiness. While such information is produced by most risk-management information systems, the degree to which that information is drawn upon in reports to trading counterparties still varies widely.

Given the limitations of the typical financial statement for timely assessment of a hedge fund's trading risks, banks and securities firms supplement traditional financial analysis with occasional on-site visits and qualitative evaluations of the fund's risk management practices, trading strategies, and performance. Such qualitative evaluations, however, may not eliminate counterparties' need for better quantitative information.

Collateral practices

Because of the difficulties of assessing the creditworthiness of hedge funds, counterparties typically use collateral as a risk mitigation device. Generally, unsecured credit extension occurs only if sufficient information is available to assure the creditor that the borrower's credit risk is low. In practice, the degree of collateralization tends to vary with the creditworthiness of the borrower. For higher-risk counterparties, or counterparties for which credit related information is unavailable or too costly to acquire, credit exposures are more likely to be collateralized. A trading counterparty may be asked to post collateral if the current credit exposure rises, or if the creditworthiness of the counterparty deteriorates. In addition, collateral may be required to cover the potential future exposure either at inception or upon subsequent periodic review.

While collateral can mitigate credit risk in trading relationships, it does not eliminate it. For example, the liquidity support provided to a hedge fund may be withdrawn during periods of stress when it is most needed. This vulnerability of the fund, in turn, can affect other hedge fund counterparties, especially those that use collateral to control credit risk. In other words, the requirement to cover the mark-to-market exposure with collateral can foster a false sense of

---

[11] Bank for International Settlements, *Public Disclosure of Market and Credit Risks by Financial Intermediaries*, September 1994.

security because a hedge fund's ability to post collateral may evaporate, leaving the counterparty that relies on collateral with the unsatisfactory prospect of liquidating positions in a declining market. Thus, counterparties typically use collateral in conjunction with other methods of credit exposure management.

While collateral is now used to a greater degree than in the past, before last fall, greater competition for hedge fund business by banks and securities firms appeared to have loosened collateral terms and conditions. In many cases, banks and securities firms did not require collateral for potential future exposure. In addition, one-way collateral agreements in which the hedge fund was required to post collateral to the dealer, but not vice versa, gave way to reciprocal collateral agreements where either party could be required to post collateral, depending on the direction of the credit exposure. Such arrangements were typical only for the more established market participants.

More recently, because of the information problems associated with hedge funds and the volatility of hedge fund net asset values, banks and securities firms now usually require collateral on their exposures to hedge fund customers. Generally, collateral is required to cover the current credit exposure or current replacement value. Even though the option to make daily collateral calls exists, to reduce the need for frequent small transfers of collateral, some business is conducted on a loss-threshold basis under which additional collateral is not required until a certain replacement value amount is exceeded. The current exposure thresholds that trigger collateral calls are usually small, however, and current replacement values are generally well collateralized.

Credit limits

Credit limits on counterparty exposures are an important credit-risk management tool that serve to control credit-risk exposures through diversification. Like other sources of credit risk for banks and securities firms, credit exposures to hedge funds arising from both trading activities and direct lending are subject to credit limits. Credit limits may take the form of an overall limit across all product and business lines, and sub-limits may be applied at the level of individual products. Limits may also be applied at the industry level — for instance, to hedge funds as a group.

The size of a credit limit imposed by a creditor is based upon the counterparty's creditworthiness, and limits are applied to hedge funds as determined by an assessment of their relative returns and risks. The adequacy of spreads relative to the risks involved, compared to other business opportunities, plays a role in the dialogue between business units and the risk-management function in the setting of credit and trading limits.

The nature of the credit exposure, such as the maturity, or whether secured or unsecured, is also a factor in determining the size of a credit limit. In addition, when netting arrangements are enforceable, a credit limit may be applied to the net exposure as well as the gross amount. The metric in which the exposure is measured can be a nominal amount, the current market value, or a measure of potential exposure. Depending on the products comprising the exposure, the limit may be applied to a combination of all three measures.

Monitoring

Monitoring of credit exposures is an important part of credit-risk management. This monitoring may cover both an on-going assessment of the counterparty's financial condition as well as monitoring the status of the current exposure. The monitoring systems include on-going financial reporting requirements, as well as daily mark-to-market valuation of exposures.

The daily monitoring of exposures and the active management of exposure and collateral levels can help control the credit risk in a trading relationship. For example, some warning of problems may be inferred if a customer's ability to post collateral becomes irregular. Such procedures may identify potential problems, allowing timely adjustment of trading and credit limits, or in an extreme case, a more orderly unwinding of positions.

For the assessment of changes in the financial condition of a counterparty, monitoring of exposures provides only a partial view of a hedge fund's condition because a dealer's own transactions with the hedge fund might not reveal the fund's overall risk profile.

THE LTCM EPISODE

A. Background

Long-Term Capital Management, L.P. ("LTCM") was founded in early 1994. Although LTCM itself is a Delaware limited partnership with its main offices in Connecticut, the fund that it operates, Long-Term Capital Portfolio, L.P., ("the LTCM Fund," or "the Fund") is a Cayman Islands partnership.[12] LTCM sought to profit from a variety of trading strategies, including convergence trades[13] and dynamic hedging.[14] LTCM's principals included individuals with substantial reputations in the financial markets and especially in the economic theory of financial markets. From its inception, LTCM had a prominent position in the community of hedge funds, both because of the reputation of its principals, and also because of its large initial capital stake.

---

[12] The LTCM Fund was the investment vehicle for a number of feeder funds, which were structured to meet the tax, regulatory, or accounting concerns of different classes of investors from different countries.

[13] Convergence trading (also sometimes known as relative value arbitrage) refers to the practice of taking offsetting positions in two related securities in the hopes that the price gap between the two securities will move in a favorable direction. In some cases, there is an underlying reason why the favorable relative price changes are thought to be inevitable, while in others the trade is more purely speculative.

[14] Dynamic hedging refers to the practice of managing nonlinear price risk exposure (*i.e.*, from options) through active rebalancing of underlying positions, rather than by arranging offsetting hedges directly.

The LTCM Fund produced returns, net of fees, of approximately 40 percent in 1995 and 1996, and slightly less than 20 percent in 1997. At the end of 1997, LTCM returned approximately $2.7 billion in capital to its investors, reducing the capital base of the fund by about 36 percent to $4.8 billion. Despite this reduction in its capital base, however, the hedge fund apparently did not reduce the scale of its investment positions. Put another way, the managers of the Fund decided to increase its balance-sheet leverage by reducing its capital base rather than by increasing its positions.

Approximately 80 percent of the LTCM Fund's balance-sheet positions were in government bonds of the G-7 countries (*viz.*, the United States, Canada, France, Germany, Italy, Japan, and the United Kingdom). Nevertheless, the Fund was active in many other markets, including securities markets, exchange-traded futures, and OTC derivatives. Its activity was also geographically diverse, encompassing markets in North America, Europe, and Asia. Specifically:

- The LTCM Fund participated in government bond markets, mortgage-backed securities markets, corporate bond markets, emerging bond markets, and equity markets. The LTCM Fund held long and short positions in these markets, and supported these positions in many cases through repo and reverse repo agreements and securities lending agreements with a large number of other market participants.

- The LTCM Fund took on futures positions at about a dozen major futures exchanges worldwide, including some very sizable positions. These were primarily concentrated in two areas — interest rate (including bond) futures and equity index futures.

- The LTCM Fund engaged in OTC derivatives contracts with several dozen counterparties. These positions included swap, forward, and option contracts, and were predominantly focused on interest rates and equity markets.

- The LTCM Fund participated in the foreign exchange markets to support its activities in multiple national markets. Although the Fund sometimes held open foreign exchange positions, it was not substantially engaged in efforts to profit from foreign exchange fluctuations.

- The LTCM Fund's involvement in the markets for physical commodities, if any, was negligible.

Overall, the distinguishing features of the LTCM Fund were the scale of its activities, the large size of its positions in certain markets, and the extent of its leverage, both in terms of balance-sheet measures and on the basis of more meaningful measures of risk exposure in relation to capital. The Fund reportedly had over 60,000 trades on its books, including long securities positions of over $50 billion and short positions of an equivalent magnitude. At the end of August, 1998, the gross notional amounts of the Fund's contracts on futures exchanges exceeded

$500 billion, swaps contracts more than $750 billion, and options and other OTC derivatives over $150 billion.

Moreover, the Fund held large relative positions in several markets, such as in U.S. and foreign futures exchanges. For example, a number of the Fund's futures positions represented more than five percent of open interest, and in a few cases, well above ten percent. Relative to daily turnover in those markets, the scale of the fund's positions were even larger. In addition, the LTCM Fund also held very significant positions in specific securities.

With regard to leverage, the LTCM Fund's balance sheet on August 31, 1998, included over $125 billion in assets. Even using the January 1, 1998, equity capital figure of $4.8 billion, this level of assets still implies a balance-sheet leverage ratio of more than 25-to-1. The extent of this leverage implies a great deal of risk. Although exact comparisons are difficult, it is likely that the LTCM Fund's exposure to certain market risks was several times greater than that of the trading portfolios typically held by major dealer firms.

The LTCM Fund's size and leverage, as well as the trading strategies that it utilized, made it vulnerable to the extraordinary financial market conditions that emerged following Russia's devaluation of the ruble and declaration of a debt moratorium on August 17 of last year. Russia's actions sparked a "flight to quality" in which investors avoided risk and sought out liquidity. As a result, risk spreads and liquidity premiums rose sharply in markets around the world. The size, persistence, and pervasiveness of the widening of risk spreads confounded the risk management models employed by LTCM and other participants. Both LTCM and other market participants suffered losses in individual markets that greatly exceeded what conventional risk models, estimated during more stable periods, suggested were probable. Moreover, the simultaneous shocks to many markets confounded expectations of relatively low correlations between market prices and revealed that global trading portfolios like LTCM's were less well diversified than assumed. Finally, the "flight to quality" resulted in a substantial reduction in the liquidity of many markets, which, contrary to the assumptions implicit in their models, made it difficult to reduce exposures quickly without incurring further losses.

B. LTCM's Near Failure

On July 31, 1998, the LTCM Fund held $4.1 billion in capital, down about fifteen percent from the beginning of the year. During the single month of August, the LTCM Fund suffered additional losses of $1.8 billion, bringing the loss of equity for the year to over fifty percent. The Fund's capital base was now $2.3 billion, and LTCM reported to investors that it was seeking an injection of capital.

During the first two weeks of September 1998, concern about LTCM was a major topic of conversation in the financial markets. The LTCM Fund suffered substantial further losses and found it difficult to reduce its positions because of the large size of those positions. In addition, as its condition deteriorated, previously flexible credit arrangements became more rigid and the daily mark-to-market valuations for collateral calls by counterparties became more contentious. These factors added to the liquidity pressures facing LTCM.

By Friday, September 18, these liquidity pressures, together with continuing declines in the Fund's capital, were causing serious concerns among the Fund's principals about the ability of the Fund to continue meeting its cash flow obligations in the event of further shocks to its market value. As LTCM's efforts to raise new capital remained unsuccessful, its condition was also a source of major concern to numerous market participants. These market participants were concerned about the possibility that LTCM could abruptly collapse in the very near term and about the consequences that such a collapse might have on what already were extremely fragile world markets.

By September 21, the LTCM Fund's liquidity situation was bleak. Bear Stearns, LTCM's prime brokerage firm, had required LTCM to collateralize potential settlement exposures, reducing the fund's overall liquidity resources. LTCM's repo and OTC derivatives counterparties were seeking as much collateral as possible through the daily margining process, in many cases by seeking to apply possible liquidation values to mark-to-market valuations. The cash-flow strains were raising the risk that the LTCM Fund would be unable to meet payments due at the end of September. Moreover, in the absence of additional injections of liquidity, further unfavorable market movements could have led to a default as soon as Wednesday, September 23. Thus, a very short period of time remained for the participants to explore resolution alternatives. While LTCM's plight had been known to some market participants to varying degrees, no one had as yet stepped forward to offer an alternative that would avoid a default.

The primary trading counterparties and creditors to the LTCM Fund were themselves the firms most exposed in a default scenario. These firms had played an important role in allowing LTCM to build up such large positions. The self-interest of these firms was to find an alternative resolution that cost less than they could expect to lose in the event of default.

On Tuesday, September 22, a Core Group of four of the most concerned counterparties began seriously exploring the possibility of mutually beneficial alternatives to default. The main alternative the Core Group focused on came to be known as the consortium approach and involved the recapitalization of the LTCM Fund through mutual investments by its major counterparties in a recently set up feeder fund and a relatively small investment in a newly set up limited liability company which became a new general partner of the LTCM Fund. Under this approach, the stake of the original owners would be written down to 10 percent and the consortium would acquire the remaining 90 percent ownership share, as well as operational control of LTCM.

Following lengthy discussions in the afternoon and evening of September 23, fourteen firms agreed to participate in the consortium. The Federal Reserve Bank of New York provided the facilities for these discussions and encouraged the firms involved to seek the least disruptive solution that they believed was in their own collective self-interest. The agreement was reached only after the firms involved became convinced that no other alternative to default was possible. The agreement followed the unraveling of a last minute alternative resolution which was presented to LTCM late in the morning of September 23. Another investor group had offered to purchase LTCM's portfolio, and at that time, all discussions related to the consortium approach were suspended. The consortium discussions reconvened only after it became clear that this alternative would not take place.[15]

The firms participating in the consortium invested about $3.6 billion in new equity in the fund, and in return received a 90 percent equity stake in LTCM's portfolio along with operational control. The responsibility and burden of resolving LTCM's difficulties remained with the counterparties that had allowed the hedge fund to build up its positions in the first place. The principals and investors in LTCM suffered very substantial losses on their equity stakes in the fund when their claim was reduced to ten percent.

C. The LTCM Fund Achieved Extraordinary Levels of Leverage and Risk

Assessed against the trading practices of hedge funds and other trading institutions discussed above — namely, mark-to-market, leverage, and active trading — and disclosure and monitoring requirements, the LTCM Fund stood out with respect to its opaqueness and low degree of external monitoring, and its high degree of leverage. At the time of its near-failure, the LTCM Fund was the most highly leveraged large hedge fund reporting to the CFTC. The combination of LTCM Fund's large capital base and high degree of leverage allowed it to hold more than $125 billion in total assets, nearly four times the assets of the next largest hedge fund. LTCM then faced severe market liquidity problems when its investments began losing value and the fund attempted to unwind some of its positions. The liquidity problems faced by LTCM were compounded by the large size of its positions in certain markets.

Although its mark-to-market valuations called LTCM's managers' attention to the Fund's problems well before the Fund's net worth was exhausted, individual counterparties — partly because there were so many — were not necessarily aware of the depth of LTCM's liquidity problems. Neither were the balance sheet and income statements that LTCM provided to its counterparties very informative about the Fund's risk profile and concentration of exposures in certain markets. This opaqueness of LTCM's risk profile is an important part of the LTCM story and raises a number of concerns regarding credit-risk management and counterparty trading relationships.

First, the LTCM Fund was able to acquire positions that proved large enough to strain its ability to manage the resulting market and liquidity risks. An issue here is whether the LTCM Fund's investors and counterparties were aware of the nature of the exposures and risks the hedge

---

[15] This alternative offer is described more fully by William J. McDonough, President of the Federal Reserve Bank of New York, in his statement and subsequent testimony before the House Committee on Banking and Financial Services, during its October 1, 1998, hearing on hedge fund operations.

fund had accumulated, such as the Fund's exposure to market liquidity and funding liquidity risks. They almost certainly were not adequately aware since, by most accounts, they exercised minimal scrutiny of the Fund's risk-management practices and risk profile.

This insufficient monitoring arose, in part, because of LTCM's practice of disclosing only minimal information to these parties, information such as balance sheet and income statements that did not reveal meaningful details about the Fund's risk profile and concentration of exposures in certain markets. In LTCM's case, this minimal level of disclosure was tolerated because of the stature of its principals, its impressive track record, and the opportunity for the Fund's investors and counterparties to profit from a significant relationship with LTCM. LTCM's willingness to bear risk also made it an attractive counterparty for those firms seeking to hedge their own exposures. Thus, the main limitation on the LTCM Fund's overall scale and leverage was that provided by its managers and principals.

A related concern is whether the LTCM Fund's counterparties were lulled into a false sense of security based solely upon their collateral arrangements with the Fund. Counterparties' current credit exposures were in most cases covered by collateral. However, their potential future exposures were likely not adequately assessed, priced, or collateralized relative to the potential price shocks the markets were facing at the end of September 1998, and relative to the creditworthiness of the LTCM Fund at that time. Further, expectations about the ability to collect on collateral calls were probably unrealistic for an entity like the LTCM Fund, particularly in the market environment of last Fall. Thus, counterparties that were relying on variation margin to manage credit risk were left with the unsatisfactory prospect of liquidating collateral and closing out exposures in a declining market.

A further issue concerns the degree to which the management of credit risk in trading relationships should take account of the link between market risk, liquidity risk, and credit risk. The fall-out from recent market shocks shows the need to go beyond value-at-risk and potential future exposure models built only on very recent price data that may underestimate both the size of potential shocks to risk factors and their correlation. It appears that some of the risk models used by LTCM *and* its creditors and counterparties were flawed.

While nearly all major trading firms make use of risk-measurement models to estimate the amount of risk being assumed, the decision about how much estimated risk can be safely borne for each dollar of capital is one that depends ultimately on the judgment of the firm's managers. Although it is not known how large a margin of error LTCM's principals allowed for in their estimates of the risks they were assuming, it is clear that LTCM's models underestimated the risk they were taking and the effect of their own positions in markets. Prior to this episode, LTCM maintained that the LTCM Fund's positions embodied risk similar to that of investing in the S&P 500 index on an unleveraged basis but were essentially uncorrelated with equity returns. LTCM's creditors and counterparties may have accepted this contention or had risk models which produced similar results.

Although individual counterparties imposed bilateral trading limits on their own activities with LTCM, none of its investors, creditors, or counterparties provided an effective check on its overall activities. Thus, the only limitation on the LTCM Fund's overall scale and leverage was that provided by its managers/principals. From their perspective, the desire to maximize returns (and management fees) on each dollar of invested capital naturally created an incentive to increase leverage. In this setting, the principals, making use of internal risk models, determined the frontier for safe operation of the fund.

A point whose significance was apparently missed by LTCM and its counterparties and creditors was that, while LTCM was diversified across global markets, it was not very well diversified as to strategy. It was betting in general that liquidity, credit and volatility spreads would narrow from historically high levels. When the spreads widened instead in markets across the world, LTCM found itself at the brink of insolvency. In retrospect, it can be seen that LTCM and others underestimated the likelihood that liquidity, credit and volatility spreads would move in a similar fashion in markets across the world at the same time.

Moreover, not only did liquidity, credit and volatility spreads widen, but the liquidity of many markets dried up. This compounded the problem faced by LTCM's creditors, because a liquidation of LTCM's positions would have been disorderly and could have had adverse market effects on their positions and that of many other market participants. The possibility of this situation occurring was not fully considered by either LTCM or its creditors.

This raises the issue of how events that are assumed to be extreme and very improbable should be incorporated into risk-management and business practice, and how they should be dealt with by public policy. The risk management weaknesses revealed by the LTCM episode were not unique to LTCM and its creditors and counterparties. Financial market participants have made significant progress in recent years in strengthening risk-management capabilities. Nevertheless, as new technology has fostered a major expansion in the volume and, in some cases, the leverage of transactions, some existing risk models have underestimated the probability of severe losses. This shows the need for ensuring that decisions about the appropriate level of capital for risky positions become an issue that is explicitly considered; when outlier events are omitted from risk models, such decisions are made by default. While newer models are endeavoring to reflect such new realities more accurately and realistically, policy initiatives that are aimed at simply reducing default likelihoods to extremely low levels might be counterproductive if they unnecessarily disrupt trading activity and the intermediation of risks that support the financing of real economic activity.

The larger issue raised by LTCM is how to enhance the robustness of trading activity. Specific concerns include how to constrain the build-up of fragile positions with excessive exposure to risk without impeding trading activity that is needed to provide liquidity and absorb market shocks. Better credit discipline in trading relationships can help in both of these areas. First, improvement in credit discipline can prevent the build-up of large or concentrated exposures whose liquidation might destabilize markets, as appeared to have happened in the case of LTCM.

16

Second, better information about counterparties can reduce the likelihood of surprises about a trader, and make a destabilizing pulling back by counterparties less likely. Beyond changes in risk appetites that cause investors to withdraw from markets, doubts about a trader's creditworthiness also can impair the trader's ability to continue trading during periods of market turmoil. Thus, greater confidence about credit exposures in trading relationships will strengthen the ability of markets to withstand shocks.

One consideration regarding the possible approaches to managing the credit risk problem is that each has different costs and liquidity implications for different types of traders. In addition, market participants also have diverse levels of creditworthiness. Thus, the costs and benefits of alternative credit-risk control arrangements are different across market participants, and such differences probably should be taken into account in policy initiatives.

D. Counterparty Losses and Market Disruptions That May Have Resulted from a Default of LTCM

A default by the LTCM Fund would have caused counterparties to move quickly to limit their exposures. These risk-limiting moves may have required the liquidation or replacement of positions and collateral in the many markets where the LTCM Fund held sizable positions at depressed prices. These very actions in a market that, last September, was already suffering from a substantial reduction in liquidity could have resulted in significant losses. LTCM itself estimated that its top 17 counterparties would have suffered various substantial losses — potentially between $3 billion and $5 billion in aggregate — and shared this information with the fourteen firms participating in the consortium. The firms in the consortium saw that their losses could be serious, with potential losses to some firms amounting to $300 million to $500 million each. Moreover, if the LTCM Fund had defaulted last September, the losses, market disruptions, and the pronounced lack of liquidity could have been more severe if not for the use of closeout, netting, and collateral provisions.

LTCM's trading activities and counterparties

LTCM's counterparties and the assets that they traded included the following.

Prime Broker. Like most hedge funds, LTCM centralized much of its custodial, recordkeeping, clearance, and financing services with a single firm. This bundle of services is typically referred to as prime brokerage and generally includes the following: providing intraday credit to facilitate foreign exchange payments and securities transactions; providing margin credit to finance purchases of equity securities; and borrowing securities from investment fund managers on behalf of hedge funds to support the hedge funds' short positions (thus allowing investment funds to avoid direct exposure to hedge funds). LTCM's prime broker was, and still is, Bear Stearns.

Futures clearing firms. At the time of the LTCM Fund's near failure, Bear Stearns also served as a clearing firm for LTCM's U.S. exchange-traded futures activity, while Merrill Lynch was the clearing firm for its trades on foreign futures exchanges. As such, the role of these clearing firms was to guarantee LTCM's positions with the relevant futures clearinghouses, thus bearing significant credit exposure to the LTCM Fund. Both Bear Stearns and Merrill Lynch required LTCM to post customer margin required by the futures exchanges, including both initial margin and, to cover the changing mark-to-market value of the LTCM Fund's futures positions, daily variation margin.

Repo and reverse repo counterparties. The LTCM Fund conducted repo and reverse repo transactions on U.S. and other government securities with approximately seventy-five counterparties.

OTC derivatives counterparties. The LTCM Fund engaged in OTC derivative transactions with about fifty counterparties. In most cases, the current mark-to-market exposure was collateralized. Some counterparties were even holding collateral to offset potential future exposure. In some cases, the LTCM Fund held very substantial OTC derivatives positions related to reference assets that were not actively traded. There was little liquidity in these specific instruments, even under normal circumstances.

Loan counterparties. For liquidity management, LTCM had arranged for syndicated credit facilities involving several dozen banks. Much of the credit available was not drawn on until the time of the near-collapse of the fund, however, and was not a major factor in the fund's build up of leverage.

Market liquidity in September 1998 and potential effects of an LTCM default

In assessing the effect of an LTCM default in late September 1998, it is helpful to recall that the market turmoil of the summer (and particularly August) had already caused sizable trading losses at many financial firms. These losses led to a general pullback in firms' willingness to take on risk positions and was evident in the "flight to quality" observed during this period. A severe decline in overall market liquidity was apparent in increased levels of excess bank reserves and a decline in repo and reverse repo positions — both indicative of a desire among firms to conserve liquidity. LTCM itself experienced substantial difficulty in reducing the LTCM Fund's risk positions during this period, even though it was not attempting to reduce all of its positions at the same time.

As noted above, the LTCM Fund held a great variety of relatively large positions with numerous trading partners. Those positions, combined with the market volatility and lack of liquidity might have led to a series of dramatic and punishing events for LTCM's trading counterparties and the markets themselves in the event of a default by the LTCM Fund.

By the time the LTCM Fund got into serious financial difficulties, Bear Stearns had ceased to provide intraday clearing credit. However, Bear Stearns was still a major securities lending counterparty with the LTCM Fund, putting it in a position similar to the Fund's repo and reverse repo counterparties. In closing out these transactions, the LTCM Fund's counterparties would have rapidly sold or purchased securities in the market. Because the cost of closing out their positions might have proved greater than the realized value of the securities or cash held as collateral by repo, reverse repo, or securities lending counterparties of the LTCM Fund, these counterparties were still exposed to losses in the event of a default by the Fund.

Like its other counterparties, the LTCM Fund's OTC derivatives counterparties would have had to re-balance their portfolios in an effort to reduce risk brought on by a default of the Fund. All of these counterparties would have needed to re-establish positions and hedges related to any contracts upon which the LTCM Fund had defaulted. The cost of closing out these positions might have proved greater than the value of the collateral ultimately realized. The risk of loss would have been particularly high for derivatives counterparties of the Fund who were exposed to illiquid risk positions that would have been even more difficult to hedge or liquidate last September.

Finally, given that their syndicated lines of credit to LTCM were largely unsecured, the providers of the credits discussed above would have lost nearly all amounts outstanding under these loans.

The effect of closeout and netting in mitigating losses

As described above, the losses suffered by the LTCM Fund's trading counterparties in the event of a default would have been considerable. This would have been true even though the U.S. Bankruptcy Code makes an exception to the automatic stay with respect to contractual rights to net and closeout positions in certain financial contracts in the event of default. However, the use of closeout and netting rights by these counterparties, which is not subject to the automatic stay, may have mitigated these losses and tempered any ensuing instability in the market. In the event of default, these rights, in general, contribute to the stability of markets as a whole by reducing the potential size of credit exposures and thus lowering the probability that the inability of one market participant to meet their obligations will cause others to be unable meet their obligations (*i.e.*, domino effects).

Closeout, or termination, refers to the right under a master agreement to terminate one or more contracts immediately upon certain specified events and to compute a termination amount due to, or due from, the defaulting party. The termination amount is generally based upon the value of the contract at the time of closeout. The ability to terminate most financial market contracts upon an event of default is central to the effective management of market risk by financial market participants like the trading counterparties of the LTCM Fund. Without these rights, parties are left with uncertainty as to whether the contracts will be performed, resulting in uncontrollable market risk. By providing for termination of a contract upon the default of a counterparty, a participant can remove uncertainty as to whether a contract will be performed, fix the value of the contract at that point, and attempt to re-hedge itself against its market risk.

Closeout goes hand in hand with netting, another valuable legal right which operates as a risk-reducing mechanism whenever a party to a financial contract defaults. Netting refers to the right to set off, or net, claims or payment obligations between two or more parties — with the goal of arriving at a single obligation that runs between these parties. Under current U.S. law, financial institutions in the United States can net and closeout a variety of financial contracts without fear that a bankruptcy court will try to reverse such procedures vis-a-vis a counterparty that has defaulted. Moreover, closeout netting in connection with financial transactions of the type undertaken by the LTCM Fund generally is exempt from being temporarily blocked by the automatic stay that usually applies upon a filing of a bankruptcy petition.

In financial transactions like those described in this section — securities lending and borrowing; futures purchases, sales, and clearing; repo and reverse transactions; and OTC derivatives contracts — netting can serve to reduce the credit exposure of counterparties to a failed debtor and thereby limit "domino failures" and systemic risk. The ability to net may also contribute to market liquidity by permitting more activity between counterparties within prudent credit limits.[16] This added liquidity can be important in minimizing market disruptions due to the failure of a market participant.

Potential market impact of disorderly liquidation

In addition to the credit losses that LTCM's creditors and counterparties would have suffered, a default also could have had broader consequences for the markets in which these firms were active. First, the liquidation and closing out of positions could have generated significant movements in market prices and rates, affecting the market value of positions held by the LTCM Fund's counterparties as well as by other market participants. Second, the resulting rush by the Fund's counterparties and others to reappraise their credit risks, coupled with an increase in uncertainty, could have exacerbated the broader decline in market liquidity, making it more difficult for market participants to manage risks. Third, those firms with exposures to LTCM could have encountered increased concerns about their own credit standing, with a resulting rise in their cost of obtaining funds.

The LTCM Fund's counterparties and creditors were facing the risk posed by the impact of a default by the LTCM Fund in the unusual market environment prevailing in late September. By that time, worldwide investor confidence had already reached a low ebb. Although markets were already operating in a low interest-rate environment, the flight to safety further reduced the

---

[16] Although an individual counterparty's gross positions with the LTCM Fund might arguably have been smaller if they had been unable to rely on netting, this may not mean that the Fund's gross positions would have been significantly smaller. It is possible that the LTCM Fund would have assumed the same gross positions by dealing with more counterparties.

yield on the longest-maturity U.S. Treasury bond to a thirty year low on Friday, September 18. During the previous month, interest rate spreads had widened substantially, while equity markets around the world had suffered significant declines. The level of economic uncertainty as measured by market volatility had risen while liquidity was declining. Finally, most major market participants had already suffered significant trading losses during August and September, and were anxious to avoid further losses.

In the midst of these extraordinary market conditions, a default by the LTCM Fund could have had effects different from a default during less unsettled market conditions. The LTCM Fund's counterparties would have had to manage the effects of the direct credit losses from the default as well as further indirect effects if the default accelerated a flight to safety and liquidity that was already occurring.

Effects of the use of collateral by LTCM's trading partners

The parties to many of the transactions referred to in this section often rely on collateral from their counterparties. Current credit exposure under OTC contracts can be collateralized, current exposures under securities lending, repo, and reverse repo transactions are in effect collateralized, and the use of margin in futures trading is a form of collateral-taking. The right to liquidate assets held as collateral without judicial approval in the event of a bankruptcy is very important to the preservation of liquidity among financial market participants. Together with closeout rights and netting, the use of collateral can effectively reduce current credit risk in financial contracts.

However, there can be limits to the benefits of using collateral. Those firms relying on collateral posted by LTCM, particularly the counterparties to OTC derivatives trades with the LTCM Fund, generally did not demand collateral based upon calculations of potential future exposure. If its collateral holdings did not reflect potential future exposure, then a firm selling collateral provided by LTCM in the event of a default would still have been exposed to the difference between the value of the collateral and the value of the closed-out financial contract at the time the collateral was sold. Given how much financial markets can shift — and the extremely unsettled market conditions last September — these types of losses could have been considerable in the event the LTCM Fund had defaulted on its obligations.

When illiquid assets are posted as collateral, they can be difficult to sell in the event of a default, particularly in times of market stress. This probably would not have been the case with LTCM, given that much of the collateral pledged by the firm consisted of government securities for which there was a very liquid market. However, as is discussed later in this report, in the event the LTCM Fund had declared bankruptcy in its chartering jurisdiction, the Cayman Islands, there is some legal uncertainty as to whether the rights of its counterparties to liquidate collateral under the U.S. Bankruptcy Code would have been delayed. This may have provided a further incentive to the LTCM Fund's creditors to avoid a bankruptcy scenario. (An amendment to the

U.S. Bankruptcy Code proposed by the Working Group would create a sounder legal basis for relying on the right to liquidate collateral in future such cases.)

II. PUBLIC POLICY ISSUES

Leverage and Risk

The public policy issue raised by market participants' use of leverage is, first, determining the proper balance between the benefit leverage confers to markets and the potential systemic risk posed by high levels of leverage. If it is determined that, from time to time, existing mechanisms do not adequately limit the use of leverage, resulting in unacceptably high levels of systemic risk, then the question becomes one of how best to address this concern.

Leverage allows an investor to take on higher risks, including those risks that are shed by others. Thus, the leveraged exposure of investors with higher risk appetites can be a vehicle that allows a larger number of risk-averse investors to reduce their risks. While the leverage that supports the reallocation of risk provides benefits, it can be fragile. In a volatile market, high levels of leverage increase the likelihood that a leveraged entity will fail, in part because the size of potential losses can seriously deplete and even wipe out the entity's net worth.

When leveraged investors are overwhelmed by market or liquidity shocks, the risks they have assumed will be discharged back into the market. Thus, highly leveraged investors have the potential to exacerbate instability in the market as a whole. The outcome may be direct losses inflicted on creditors and trading counterparties, as well as an indirect impact on other market participants through price changes resulting from the disappearance of investors willing to bear higher risks. The indirect impact is potentially the more serious effect. Volatility and sharp declines in asset prices can heighten uncertainty about credit risk and disrupt the intermediation of credit. These secondary effects, if not contained, could cause a contraction of credit and liquidity, and ultimately, heighten the risk of a contraction in real economic activity.

The leverage employed by hedge funds is acquired through derivatives transactions, repurchase agreements, short sales, and direct financing. In probably all cases, these exposures are collateralized at current market value. However, in the case of LTCM, the potential future exposure was not adequately collateralized relative to the creditworthiness of the LTCM Fund or to the potential price shocks the markets were facing in September 1998.

Banks and securities firms have viewed hedge funds as desirable trading customers. For instance, dealers earn trading revenue from the funds' transactions flows without directly bearing the risks undertaken by the funds. Hedge funds' willingness to take on risks also may make it easier for dealers to execute hedging transactions to shed unwanted risks. Competition for hedge fund business may have led to a gradual erosion of risk management practices with regard to some hedge fund customers, and certainly with respect to the LTCM Fund in particular.

A. Measuring Leverage and Risk

Placing direct constraints on leverage presents certain difficulties. Given investors' diverse exposures to risk, and differences in their links to other market participants, requiring a uniform degree of balance-sheet leverage for all investors does not seem reasonable. First, balance-sheet leverage by itself is not an adequate measure of risk. For any given leverage ratio, the fragility of a portfolio depends on the market, credit, and liquidity risks in the portfolio. In addition, a high capital requirement based on balance-sheet concepts alone might induce fund managers to shift their risk-taking activities to more speculative trading strategies as they seek to meet rate-of-return targets on the required capital. It could also induce managers to move to off-balance-sheet risk-taking strategies such as through the use of derivatives.

An alternative measure to balance-sheet leverage is the ratio of potential gains and losses relative to net worth, such as value-at-risk relative to net worth. An advantage of such a statistical measure is its ability to produce a more meaningful description of leverage in terms of risk. A disadvantage is the potential pitfalls in measuring value-at-risk, such as through faulty or incomplete modeling assumptions or narrow time horizons. These issues suggest that enforcing a meaningful regulatory capital requirement or leverage ratio for a wide and diverse range of investment funds would be a difficult undertaking.

An alternative tool for indirectly influencing excessive leverage is credit-risk management. Credit-risk management can help to constrain the leverage employed by significant market participants, including hedge funds, thereby reducing systemic risk. The diversity of the credit risk and liquidity profiles of borrowers has led creditors to use a variety of tools to control credit risk. Public policy initiatives relating to hedge funds should build upon those practices that have worked well, and should encourage their use and improvements in their implementation.

Collateral, capital, information, and the price of credit. Collateralization and the use of credit-risk spreads on credit exposures, including trading exposures, offer alternative ways of managing these same types of credit risk. The method which is chosen typically depends on the relative costs to the customer of the collateral and the credit spread that provide equivalent compensation to the creditor for the credit risk.[17] With collateralization, collateral provided by the borrower provides protection to the lender against losses from default. When credit-risk spreads are used, the lender's capital and loan-loss reserves provide protection against losses from default, and the credit spread on the loan provides compensation to the lender for the cost of capital and reserves, plus a risk premium. For customers who can easily provide information demonstrating their creditworthiness, credit may be acquired on an unsecured basis because the credit risk spread is of lower cost than the cost of providing collateral. Supervisors and regulators of banks and securities firms usually have not interfered in private choices regarding different

---

[17] For a commercial property developer, providing the property as collateral is typically cheaper than paying the unsecured credit risk spread, while for a highly creditworthy corporate borrower, issuing unsecured notes may be cheaper than providing collateral.

approaches to managing credit risk, as long as prudential standards are satisfied. For instance, in regulatory bank capital requirements, collateralized derivatives exposures have lower capital requirements than uncollateralized exposures, but the decision to collateralize has remained with the counterparties to the transaction.[18]

Tradeoff between credit and liquidity risk. Another example of the diversity in credit risk management practice is in the use of variation margin. Variation margin can reduce the credit exposure in a derivative transaction, but only at the cost of imposing higher liquidity risk on the counterparties. For highly creditworthy counterparties, the cash-flow management demands of daily variation margin can impose costs that exceed the benefit from credit risk reduction. For other counterparties, however, the benefits of lower credit risk resulting from variation margin may exceed the costs imposed by higher liquidity risk. Thus, allowing diversity in credit-risk management practices can result in a more efficient financial system.

B. Private Counterparty Discipline and Government Regulation

The primary mechanism that regulates risk-taking by firms in a market economy is the market discipline provided by creditors, counterparties (including financial contract counterparties), and investors. In principle, if a firm seeks to assume greater risks, either by increasing the riskiness of its assets or by increasing its leverage, creditors will respond by increasing the cost or reducing the availability of credit to the firm. The rising cost or reduced availability of funds provides a powerful economic incentive for firms to constrain their risk-taking.

Counterparty discipline can serve as an effective tool to mitigate the risks of excessive leverage. The constraint on leverage imposed through counterparty credit terms can occur directly through trading and credit limits or initial margin, and indirectly through credit spreads on transactions that would lower the returns from leveraged positions. The exercise of credit discipline in trading relationships has the potential to provide a balance between the benefits and risks of leverage. The counterparty's assessment of its ability to shoulder the credit exposure to the leveraged entity should constrain leverage below excessive levels. Such counterparty discipline, however, failed to constrain leverage adequately in the case of LTCM.

Such market discipline tends to be effective when creditors have the incentives and the means to evaluate the riskiness of the firm to adjust credit terms accordingly. In some cases, however, either the incentives or the means are lacking. Incentives will be reduced or eliminated if creditors do not perceive themselves to be adversely affected by increases in the firm's level of risk. In particular, if the firm's obligations are guaranteed by a financially strong third party (*e.g.*, a government), its creditors may be indifferent to its level of risk. If the firm is able to obtain

---

[18] This decentralized approach to managing credit risk, overall, has worked reasonably well. At the end of 1998, for example, total credit losses from OTC derivatives at US banks were only 0.21 of a percentage point of the average outstanding credit exposure for the year. In 1997, the figure was less than 0.05 of a percentage point.

financing from unsophisticated creditors — for example, from retail investors — those creditors may not have the means to accurately evaluate the firm's riskiness and, therefore, may not insist on credit terms commensurate with the firm's level of risk.

Even when creditors have the incentives and means to provide market discipline, risk-taking will not always be effectively constrained. Evaluation of the riskiness of firms is inherently difficult, and errors in evaluation and/or judgement are probable. Thus, business failures and losses to creditors will occur. In general, however, the failures and losses that have occurred have been small relative to the benefits of a market economy.

Consequently, in our market-based economy, market discipline of risk taking is the rule and government regulation is the exception. Generally, government regulation becomes necessary because of market failure or the failure of the pricing mechanism to account for all social costs. Government regulation of markets is largely achieved by regulating financial intermediaries that have access to the federal safety net, that play a central dealer role, or that raise funds from the general public. Any resort to government regulation should have a clear purpose and should be carefully evaluated in order to avoid unintended outcomes.

BANKRUPTCY ISSUES

A. Closeout Netting

The LTCM episode raises some issues involving the U.S. Bankruptcy Code. The first involves clarifying the ability of certain counterparties to exercise their rights with respect to closeout, netting, and liquidation of underlying collateral in the event of the filing of a bankruptcy petition without regard to the Bankruptcy Code's automatic stay.

These provisions, which the President's Working Group on Financial Markets urged Congress last year to expand and improve, are generally recognized to be important to market stability. They serve to reduce the likelihood that the procedure for resolving a single insolvency will trigger other insolvencies due to the creditors' inability to control their market risk. In other words, this protects the market from the systemic problem of "domino failures."

Nevertheless, in certain circumstances, a simultaneous rush by the counterparties of a defaulting market participant to replace their contracts could put pressure on market prices. To the extent that the default was due to fluctuations in market prices in these contracts, this pressure might tend to exacerbate those fluctuations, at least in the near term. This problem could be significant where the defaulting debtor had large positions relative to the size of the market.

The possibility of a debtor defaulting during volatile markets where the debtor had large positions relative to the size of certain markets was the specter created by the potential default of the LTCM Fund. In the highly volatile markets of September 1998, the failure of the LTCM

Fund would have left a number of creditors with open market positions subject to extreme volatility. Termination of those contracts would have required counterparties to replace contracts that they held with the LTCM Fund in the relatively near term. However, had termination not been available to the LTCM Fund's counterparties in the bankruptcy process, the uncertainty as to whether these contracts would be performed would have created great uncertainty and disruptions in these same markets, coupled with substantial uncontrollable market risk to the counterparties. The inability to exercise closeout netting rights could well have resulted in an even worse market situation if the LTCM Fund had filed for bankruptcy than the exercise of such rights in this situation.

B. Transnational Issues

The bankruptcy of any financial entity doing business in a number of markets around the world raises a number of legal issues that are incapable of resolution by any single country's laws or judicial policies. As such, the bankruptcy of the LTCM Fund would in all likelihood have been a drawn-out and expensive process for LTCM, any affected creditor, and any bankruptcy court. However, two amendments to the Bankruptcy Code might have led to greater legal certainty for any LTCM Fund bankruptcy proceeding in the U.S. They involve: (1) whether the "main" insolvency proceeding of hedge funds like the LTCM Fund, that are organized abroad but have substantial U.S. operations, should take place in U.S. courts under U.S. law and (2) the ability of counterparties of bankrupt foreign debtors to liquidate their U.S. collateral promptly. Both of these issues have been addressed by bankruptcy reform legislation under consideration by the U.S. Congress.

The Bankruptcy Code normally governs the bankruptcy of nonbank debtors in the United States. However, like many hedge funds, the LTCM Fund was a partnership organized in the Cayman Islands. Although the management of the Fund was effected through a Delaware limited partnership located in Connecticut — a separate entity called Long-Term Capital Management, L.P. — it is believed that the Fund itself would have sought bankruptcy protection in the Cayman Islands courts, under Cayman law. Had that been the case, any U.S. bankruptcy proceeding would likely have been ancillary to the main Cayman Islands proceeding.

Section 304 of the U.S. Bankruptcy Code ("Section 304") specifies general criteria for determining whether a U.S. bankruptcy court should defer to a foreign bankruptcy proceeding such as the one that probably would have occurred with the LTCM Fund and its affiliates. However, the Bankruptcy Code does not clearly address when a debtor's "main" insolvency proceeding must take place in the U.S. courts. In 1997, the United Nations Commission on International Trade Law ("UNCITRAL") approved a model statute establishing clear conventions to differentiate between a "main" insolvency proceeding and a "non-main" proceeding for debtors located in more than one jurisdiction, which would better facilitate the marshaling and distribution of a debtor's assets. Amendments to U.S. and foreign bankruptcy laws based on the UNCITRAL language would make it much more likely that with entities like the LTCM Fund, whose main place of business is the U.S., the U.S. bankruptcy proceeding would be the "main", and not an ancillary, bankruptcy proceeding.

If a hedge fund like the LTCM Fund were to declare bankruptcy in a non-U.S. jurisdiction like the Cayman Islands, Section 304 permits a receiver appointed by the non-U.S. court to seek an injunction (a "Section 304 Injunction") in a U.S. bankruptcy court. Among other things, the foreign receiver can try to use the injunction to freeze temporarily actions by U.S. creditors that affect the bankrupt party's U.S. assets. If LTCM had declared bankruptcy in the Cayman Islands, its Cayman receiver could have sought a Section 304 Injunction prohibiting at least temporarily the liquidation of U.S. collateral pledged by LTCM to its counterparties. Even a temporary delay in the liquidation of collateral could have had detrimental financial consequences for those parties holding that collateral.

It should be noted that when the main bankruptcy proceeding occurs in the U.S., creditors have clear rights to liquidate collateral held under a wide range of financial contracts. The weakness under current law is the treatment of collateral by U.S. entities when the U.S. proceeding is ancillary to a main proceeding taking place abroad. It is also possible that in the case of an LTCM Fund bankruptcy in the Cayman Islands, some trading counterparties of LTCM would have liquidated collateral despite a pending Section 304 Injunction favoring a Cayman receiver, litigating any resulting claims.

However, an amendment to the Bankruptcy Code recently proposed by the Working Group would likely prevent the use of the Section 304 Injunction by a foreign receiver to thwart counterparties of a bankrupt entity from selling collateral they hold from that entity, where the main bankruptcy proceeding is held outside the U.S. Enactment of this amendment would enhance the reputation of the U.S. market by providing greater legal certainty that collateral can be sold when it is needed most. Along with the previously discussed UNCITRAL-based proposal, these changes in law would likely improve the disposition of a bankruptcy of a hedge fund.

III. CONCLUSIONS AND RECOMMENDATIONS

The central public policy issue raised by the LTCM episode is how to constrain excessive leverage more effectively. As events in the summer and fall of 1998 demonstrated, the amount of leverage in the financial system, combined with aggressive risk taking, can greatly magnify the negative effects of any event or series of events. By increasing the chance that problems at one financial institution could be transmitted to other institutions, leverage can increase the likelihood of a general breakdown in the functioning of financial markets.

Although LTCM is a hedge fund, this issue is not limited to hedge funds. Other financial institutions, including some banks and securities firms, are larger, and generally more highly leveraged, than hedge funds. LTCM, with total assets of $129 billion at the end of 1997, was significantly larger than any other reporting hedge fund family at that time. Only 11 reporting hedge fund families, including LTCM, had total assets exceeding $10 billion at the end of 1997. At the end of 1998, LTCM's total assets were $89 billion. The notional amount of LTCM's total OTC derivatives position was $1.3 trillion at the end of 1997 and $1.5 trillion at the end of 1998. LTCM's balance sheet leverage was 28-to-1 at the end of 1997.

By comparison, at the end of 1998, the five largest commercial bank holding companies had total assets ranging from $261.5 billion to $617.7 billion, and the replacement value of their derivatives ranged from $20.6 billion to $61.6 billion. The five largest investment banks had total assets that ranged from $154 billion to $318 billion, and the replacement value of their derivatives ranged from $10 billion to $22 billion. In addition, six commercial bank holding companies and two investment banks had notional derivatives amounts of well over $1 trillion in December, 1998. The average balance sheet leverage of these large commercial bank holding companies and investments banks is also significant. At year-end 1998, the five largest commercial bank holding companies had an average leverage ratio of nearly 14-to-1, while the five largest investment banks' average leverage ratio was 27-to-1.

While leverage can play a positive role in our financial system, resulting in greater market liquidity, greater credit availability, and a more efficient allocation of resources in our economy, problems can arise when financial institutions are not disciplined in extending credit to their customers and counterparties. The LTCM episode well illustrates the need for all participants in our financial system, not only hedge funds, to face constraints in the amount of leverage they can assume.

Commercial and investment banks have more diverse sources of revenue, as well as more diverse funding sources, than hedge funds, and hence they may be more able than hedge funds to ride out periods of market turbulence. In times of market turbulence, however, banks and securities firms may have more inflexible cost structures than hedge funds, due to significantly higher fixed operating expenses, and they may also have more illiquid assets. This may tend to offset the benefits of the more diverse sources of revenues and funding enjoyed by banks and securities firms. At the same time, banks, broker-dealers, and futures commission merchants

("FCMs") are subject to federal government oversight that addresses risk management systems, public disclosure, and capital requirements.

To constrain the leverage of both regulated and unregulated financial entities, our market-based economy relies primarily on the discipline provided by creditors, counterparties, and investors. If a firm seeks to achieve greater leverage, its creditors and counterparties ordinarily will respond by increasing the cost or reducing the availability of credit to the firm. History tells us, however, that creditors, counterparties and investors from time to time misjudge their risks, and that sometimes they become complacent in their risk assessments in an attempt to achieve higher returns. Reasons for believing in the general effectiveness of private market discipline include:

- Banks and securities firms have both the incentives and the capabilities to use risk management practices that apply effective counterparty and credit discipline to protect the capital and profitability of the firms.

- Shareholders of banks and securities firms can exert pressure on management to reduce excessive risk taking if there is adequate transparency so that investors can make assessments concerning an entity's risk taking. Hedge funds that are perceived to be taking excessive risks may face withdrawals and may have trouble attracting new investors.

- Hedge funds and other financial institutions cannot achieve significant leverage without the credit and clearing services of the large banks and securities firms that are at the center of the securities and derivatives markets.

If one looks at the history of financial markets, however, it is also true that market-based constraints can break down in good times as creditors and investors become less concerned about risk, and fail to manage risk appropriately. In the case of LTCM, market discipline seems to have largely broken down. LTCM appears to have received very generous credit terms, even though it took an exceptional degree of risk. The breakdown in market discipline was made possible by risk management weaknesses at LTCM as well as at the large banks and securities firms that were LTCM counterparties. In some cases sound policies were in place, but the pressure to generate profit seems to have caused actual practices to deviate from those policies.

Reviews by banking regulators and by the SEC indicate that financial firms did not fully understand LTCM's risk profile and that some may not have adequately contemplated the market and liquidity risks that would have arisen if LTCM had defaulted. As the complexity, volume, interrelationship, and, in some cases, the leverage of transactions increased, the existing risk management procedures underestimated the probability of severe losses.

Complacency during favorable economic times also contributed to an atmosphere which gave rise to inadequate review and excessively liberal credit terms. In this atmosphere, the incident also raised questions concerning transparency and the adequacy of disclosure by highly leveraged institutions to their investors, creditors and counterparties in the markets in which LTCM was active. In any event, many of LTCM's counterparties did not establish meaningful limits on their exposures to LTCM.

The risk management weaknesses revealed by the LTCM episode were not unique to LTCM and its creditors and counterparties. Some of these weaknesses were also evident, albeit to a lesser degree, in investment and commercial banks' dealings with other highly leveraged counterparties, including other investment and commercial banks.

Even if market participants had better information and more fully understood the risks of their investments, their motivation is to protect themselves but not the system as a whole. Every firm has an incentive to restrain its risk taking in order to protect its capital, and firm managers have an incentive to protect their own investments in the firm. No firm, however, has an incentive to limit its risk taking in order to reduce the danger of contagion for other firms.

In the immediate aftermath of the LTCM episode, banks and securities firms have tightened their credit risk management policies vis-a-vis highly leveraged institutions. The heightened emphasis on risk management occurred not only due to the problems created by the LTCM episode, but also due to the increased global market instability brought on by the debt problems in several countries and the emerging markets in general. During the last quarter of 1998, financial institutions constrained the hedge fund industry by withdrawing capital and tightening credit standards. The hedge fund industry was further constrained by its own losses on certain investments. Recently, banks and securities firms have begun to loosen their credit relationships with hedge funds by easing the tighter conditions imposed in the fourth quarter of 1998, although there has not at this time been a return to the levels witnessed in the summer of 1998.

Market history indicates that even painful lessons recede from memory with time. Some of the risks of excessive leverage and risk taking can threaten the market as a whole, and even market participants not directly involved in imprudently extending credit can be affected.

Therefore, the Working Group sees the need for the following measures:

- more frequent and meaningful information on hedge funds should be made public;

- public companies, including financial institutions, should publicly disclose additional information about their material financial exposures to significantly leveraged institutions, including hedge funds;

- financial institutions should enhance their practices for counterparty risk management;

- regulators should encourage improvements in the risk management systems of regulated entities;

- regulators should promote the development of more risk-sensitive but prudent approaches to capital adequacy;

- regulators need expanded risk assessment authority for the unregulated affiliates of broker-dealers and futures commission merchants;[19]

- the Congress should enact the provisions proposed by the President's Working Group to support financial contract netting in the United States; and

- regulators should consider stronger incentives to encourage off-shore centers to comply with international standards.

Given the nature of today's global financial markets, the Working Group believes that it will be important that similar steps are taken in other countries, where relevant.

The Working Group has also considered some possible additional actions that could be given consideration if further evidence emerges that indirect regulation of currently unregulated market participants is not working effectively to constrain leverage. These possible additional actions are described in the final section of this chapter (section 8 below), although the Working Group is not recommending any of them at this time.

1. Disclosure and Reporting

Improving transparency through enhanced disclosure to the public should help market participants make better, more informed judgments about market integrity and the creditworthiness of borrowers and counterparties.

- Currently, the scope and timeliness of information made available about the financial activities of hedge funds are limited. Hedge funds should be required to disclose additional, and more up-to-date, information to the public. For hedge funds that are commodity pools, the Commodity Pool Operator ("CPO") filings currently may provide the best vehicle for conveying this information.

    – CPOs that currently report to the CFTC and exceed a certain *de minimus* size threshold, including those who manage hedge funds, should file quarterly reports rather than annual reports. Currently, these reports are filed on an annual basis. In addition, the reports that CPOs file with the CFTC could include more meaningful and comprehensive measures of

---

[19] See footnote 23 on page 39.

market risk (*e.g.*, value-at-risk or stress test results), without requiring the disclosure of proprietary information on strategies or positions. These individual financial reports should be published.

– For hedge funds that are not currently registered as CPOs, a means for disclosure should be developed to ensure that similar financial information is provided to the public. For these hedge funds, Congress would need to enact legislation that authorizes mechanisms for disclosure. Such legislation should be solely for the purpose of promoting public disclosure. All hedge fund reporting could possibly be consolidated in a single mechanism.

– Congress should enact legislation granting any additional authority necessary to achieve these goals.

- Public companies, including financial institutions, should publicly disclose a summary of direct material exposures to significantly leveraged financial institutions. To the extent covered, these entities should be aggregated by sector (*e.g.* commercial banks, investment banks, insurance companies, hedge funds and others). Public companies' exposures to significantly leveraged financial entities, including commercial banks, investment banks, finance companies, and hedge funds, may be in the form of equity, loans, or other credit exposures. Currently, neither SEC rules nor generally accepted accounting principles directly address disclosure requirements for companies with material exposures to significantly leveraged financial institutions. The interlocking nature of the financial exposures of highly leveraged financial institutions with each other leads to the potential contagion effect of financial difficulty originating initially in one firm. Requiring public companies to disclose their direct material exposures to significantly leveraged financial entities could serve to reinforce private market discipline upon these firms.

– The proposed disclosure could be required to be incorporated in the Management's Discussion and Analysis or Description of Business in periodic financial statements. Such disclosures should be accompanied by appropriate information and analyses regarding how exposures are measured as well as the quality and diversification of exposures to highly leveraged institutions. The disclosures would be included in the periodic reports (*e.g.*, Form 10-K, Form 10-Q) filed by public companies with the SEC.

– The proposed disclosures would be expected to apply to all public companies, including non-financial public companies, that have direct exposures to significantly leveraged financial institutions, as defined, that are individually or in the aggregate (a) material to the investor's financial statements, or (b) could have a material effect on the investor's financial statements resulting from losses due to possible economic events or conditions.

– The precise nature of these regulations would be determined by the SEC, taking into account public comments through the normal rule-making process.

2. Supervisory Oversight

Banking, securities, and futures regulators should monitor and encourage improvements in the risk management systems of regulated entities. The bank regulators have recently issued new guidance on these issues. They must continue to be vigilant that this guidance is followed, including through the use of their examination authority. Banking, securities and futures regulators also need to follow market developments and practices in order to determine whether existing guidance is being followed and whether additional guidance is necessary.

- Regulators of banks, securities firms, and FCMs should ensure that they address the risk management weaknesses that have been identified. Bank regulators should draw on the analyses and recommendations of the Basle Committee on Banking Supervision's recent report outlining sound practices for banks' interactions with highly leveraged institutions. Securities and futures regulators may wish to consider drawing on the upcoming International Organization of Securities Commissions ("IOSCO") studies.

- Bank regulators should ensure that entities for which they have responsibility implement sound practices appropriate to the scale and complexity of the credit services they provide, investments they make and liabilities they incur. For example, bank regulators' guidance could address, where appropriate: the need to stress test credit, as well as market risk profiles; and the appropriateness of 100% financing on reverse repurchase agreements.

- Banks should ensure that counterparties develop meaningful measures of potential future credit exposure. These measures should be used to help set exposure limits. Supervisors should encourage banks to develop policies setting out the circumstances in which potential future exposures should be collateralized.

- The SEC should ensure that securities firms follow similar prudential practices in their counterparty and credit relationships. The SEC should also encourage securities firms to do the same with their unregulated affiliates. The CFTC should ensure that FCMs follow similar prudential practices in their counterparty and credit relationships, and encourage their unregulated affiliates to do the same.

- U.S. banking regulators have recently addressed a number of concerns by issuing guidance concerning:

  (a)   the credit approval process and ongoing monitoring of credit quality;

  (b)   limits on counterparty credit exposures and the exposure management process;

  (c)   improving procedures for estimating potential future credit exposures and stress testing; and

  (d)   the use of collateral.

- In particular, US banking regulators have recently notified banks that examiners will be looking at the following points:

  (a)   Senior management and boards of directors must understand the strengths and weaknesses of their risk measurement systems, including model risk, liquidity risk, and risk of breakdown of historical correlations among different instruments and markets.

  (b)   Senior management and boards of directors must have a realistic assessment of their tolerance for losses in adverse markets.

  (c)   The interconnection of material risks, including market, credit, and liquidity risks, needs to be integrated into credit and risk management decisions.

  (d)   Steps should be taken to minimize operational errors, such as unconfirmed trades and unsigned master agreements.

  (e)   Legal risks, including contract enforceability and uncertainties concerning different legal regimes in different countries, must be clearly understood and controlled.

  (f)   The credit standards applied with respect to trading activities should be consistent with the overall credit standards of the bank.

  (g)   The risk oversight functions of banks must possess independence, authority, expertise, and corporate stature.

- The SEC will issue non-public inspection findings to several large broker-dealers, addressing the strengths and weaknesses of their particular credit risk management structure, credit control procedures, and implementation of credit and other policies.

3. Enhanced Private Sector Practices for Counterparty Risk Management

As suppliers of credit implement improved standards, their own financial safety and soundness will be enhanced. In turn, they will impose greater discipline on borrowers.

- Financial institutions should continuously review their own risk management procedures.

- As a group, financial institutions should also draft and publish enhanced standards for risk management. Areas to be addressed should include:

    (a)   the credit approval process and ongoing monitoring of credit quality, including the availability of information on counterparties and its use in making credit decisions;

    (b)   procedures for estimating potential future credit exposures, including stress testing to gauge exposures in volatile and illiquid markets, and model validation procedures, including back-testing.

    (c)   approaches to setting limits on counterparty credit exposures;

    (d)   appropriate measurement of leverage and risk;

    (e)   approaches to limit concentration of credit exposures;

    (f)   approaches to limit concentration of exposures to particular markets;

    (g)   fuller integration in risk management practices of the connections between credit and market risks;

    (h)   procedures for exercising judgment given the inherent limitations of models;

    (i)   policies regarding the use of collateral to mitigate counterparty credit risks;

    (j)   valuation practices for derivatives and collateral;

    (k)   procedures for close-out and liquidation of contracts and collateral; and

(l)   procedures to consider legal risks in credit decisions, such as those stemming from questions concerning the legal authority of a counterparty to enter into a contract and the uncertainties arising from different jurisdictions' insolvency laws, commercial codes, and recognition of netting and termination rights.

- In this context, twelve major internationally active banks and securities firms have formed the Counterparty Risk Management Policy Group ("CRMPG"). This group is developing standards for strengthened risk management practices for banks, securities firms, and others that provide credit-based services to major counterparties in the derivatives and securities markets.

- Additionally, the International Swaps and Derivatives Association has recently (March, 1999) issued a review of collateral management practices that drew lessons from collateral managers' experiences during the LTCM episode and other recent periods of market volatility. The review set out 22 recommendations for enhancing collateral management practices and an action plan for facilitating their implementation.

- Also, the Institute of International Finance, Inc., has recently issued its "Report of the Task Force on Risk Assessment" (March, 1999).

- Private sector efforts by counterparties to collect and share credit information could be helpful (see Appendix F), consistent with the anti-trust laws.

- A group of hedge funds should draft and publish a set of sound practices for their risk management and internal controls. Such a study should discuss market risk measurement and management, liquidity risk management, identification of concentrations, stress testing, collateral management, valuation of positions and collateral, segregation of duties and internal controls, and the assessment of capital needs from the perspective of hedge funds. In addition, the study should consider how individual hedge funds could assess their performance against the sound practices for investors and counterparties.

4. Capital Adequacy

Prudential supervisors and regulators should promote the development of more risk-sensitive approaches to capital adequacy.

- The Basle Committee on Banking Supervision should proceed to revise the Capital Accord in order to align capital requirements more closely with the actual risks taken by financial institutions. These efforts include greater differentiation among claims (or instruments or counterparties) based on credit quality.

- The capital treatment applied to the credit exposure from a derivatives transaction should be similar to that of a commercial loan to the same counterparty, after taking into account the nature of any underlying collateral.

- Derivatives which have the same or almost identical market risk characteristics as the underlying instruments should have similar capital charges for such market risk. (Separate capital treatment is needed to address their credit risk.)

- Value-at-risk and other risk models should be subject to validation procedures, including rigorous back-testing, consistent with the Basle approach, in order to confirm the reliability and stability of their results.

- To determine the effect on exposures from low probability but high impact events, counterparties should conduct meaningful stress tests.

- Regulators in offshore banking centers need to be encouraged to impose internationally-agreed capital standards on banks in their jurisdictions.

- The SEC should explore more risk-sensitive approaches to capital for securities firms, building on its experience with its "broker-dealer lite" approach to capital for derivatives affiliates of broker-dealers. While alternative approaches should be explored, however, it is not the intent of this recommendation that capital requirements for broker-dealers should be reduced.

- The bank regulators and, to the extent possible under the existing regulatory scheme, the SEC, should carefully monitor the use of "double leverage," particularly where the borrowing is of a short-term nature. Borrowing by a holding company that effectively funds an equity position in a broker-dealer or bank can result in problems and lead to excessive leverage. While market discipline may serve to constrain excessive double leverage, regulators should be vigilant on this issue and take necessary steps if an institution appears to be carrying this practice beyond what prudence would suggest.

5. Expanded Risk Assessment for the Unregulated Affiliates of Broker-Dealers and Futures Commission Merchants

The current authority of the SEC, the CFTC, and the Treasury Department to require financial information about the unregulated affiliates of broker-dealers and FCMs should be enhanced to monitor the risks posed by these market participants and the highly leveraged institutions which are their counterparties.[20]

One way to improve supervision would be to enhance the SEC's and CFTC's risk assessment authority to include expanded reporting, recordkeeping, and examination authority for material unregulated affiliates of broker-dealers and FCMs, along with consistent expansion of the Treasury's authority under the Government Securities Act.[21] Although the information currently gathered from broker-dealers and FCMs relating to their major unregulated affiliates, or "Material Associated Persons" ("MAPs"), is generally useful, it should be enhanced to provide a more comprehensive picture of the potential risks that an unregulated affiliate might pose to its related firm and to the financial system.[22]

For these reasons, there should be statutory changes to grant the SEC, the CFTC and the Treasury expanded risk assessment authority over broker-dealer and FCM unregulated affiliates.[23]

- As part of their enhanced risk assessment authority, the three regulators should be authorized to require broker-dealers, FCMs, and their unregulated affiliates to report credit risk information by counterparty. The reporting of this additional information would provide a comprehensive, periodic snapshot of unregulated broker-dealer and FCM affiliates and the financial risks they pose. There is overlap in these authorities, and the agencies will cooperate in order to eliminate duplicative requirements and multiple filings of the same information.

- This expanded authority should include the ability to require recordkeeping and reporting of non-aggregated position information.

- Additional data on concentrations (based on financial instrument, region, and industry sector), trading strategies, and risk models also are necessary for effective

---

[20] The SEC has the authority to write rules to collect certain financial information from broker-dealers about significant affiliates, termed "Material Associated Persons" or "MAPs." The CFTC has similar authority to obtain information from FCMs about their MAPs. The Treasury Department has the authority to write rules requiring government securities brokers and dealers registered under Section 15C of the Exchange Act to submit information about their MAPs to the SEC.

[21] This new authority does not contemplate changing the scope of the existing authority over associated persons that are subject to examination by, or reporting requirements of, a federal banking agency.

[22] This authority does not contemplate changing the scope of the existing authority over associated persons that are subject to examination by, or reporting requirements of, a federal banking agency.

[23] On the issue of expanding risk assessment for the unregulated affiliates of broker-dealers and FCMs, Chairman Greenspan of the Federal Reserve Board declines to endorse the recommendation but, in this instance, defers to the judgment of those with supervisory responsibility.

monitoring. Concentration information for large counterparties, including hedge funds and other highly leveraged institutions, is presently unavailable to the SEC and the CFTC.

- The authority to review risk management procedures and controls conducted at the holding company level, and the ability to examine the records and controls of the holding company and its material unregulated affiliates, should also be included. The authority to compel this reporting and the opportunity to verify reported information would make the regulators' expanded risk assessment authority much more effective. The ability to inspect the books, records, risk models, and management controls of broker-dealer and FCM unregulated affiliates is necessary to ensure the reports prepared are complete and accurate. Finally, the regulators need the authority to test the risk models used by MAPs.

6. Bankruptcy Code Issues

The ability to terminate financial contracts upon a counterparty's insolvency enhances market stability. Such close-out netting limits losses to solvent counterparties and reduces systemic risk. It permits the solvent parties to replace terminated contracts without incurring additional market risk and thereby preserves liquidity. The ability to exercise close-out netting also will generally serve to prevent the failure of one entity from causing an even more serious market disruption.

The near failure of the LTCM Fund raises several issues related to the Bankruptcy Code that should be addressed. The Working Group reaffirms its support for its legislative proposal entitled the "Financial Contract Netting Improvement Act, " which was transmitted to Congress on March 16, 1998, a version of which is currently pending in Congress as Title X of H.R. 833. Specifically, the Working Group recommends:

- The improvements to the close-out netting regime for certain financial contracts proposed by the Working Group should be enacted into law. These proposals would improve the netting regime under the Bankruptcy Code by expanding and clarifying the definitions of the financial contracts eligible for netting and by explicitly allowing eligible counterparties to net across different types of contracts, such as swaps, security contracts, repos, and forward contracts.

- There should be clarification that a U.S. court would apply certain key U.S. bankruptcy law protections in an ancillary proceeding taking place in the U.S. This should also prevent the issuance of a judicial stay in an ancillary proceeding from preventing an eligible counterparty from exercising contractual termination, netting, and liquidation rights that are recognized under U.S. law. It should also prevent the possibility that a hedge fund organized offshore could file for bankruptcy abroad and then petition a U.S. court to issue an injunction preventing the immediate sale of collateral located in the U.S. supporting financial contracts eligible for netting.

- The United Nations Commission on International Trade Law ("UNCITRAL") model statute should be codified, as would be done by Title IX of H.R. 833, which establishes clear conventions to differentiate between a "main" insolvency proceeding and a "non-main" proceeding for debtors located in more than one jurisdiction. These provisions would make it more likely that the jurisdiction of a main insolvency proceeding of an offshore fund would be determined by the principal place of business of the entity rather than the jurisdiction where the entity happens to be organized or incorporated. If these provisions had been law last year, it is more likely that if the LTCM Fund had failed, the main bankruptcy proceeding would have been in the U.S. rather than the Cayman Islands.

7. Offshore Financial Centers and Tax Havens

As the United States and other industrial countries continue to strengthen regulatory standards in their own countries, it will be important that other jurisdictions strengthen their supervisory systems and standards as well to ensure that hedge funds do not take advantage of any incentives to relocate to jurisdictions that do not meet international standards. Likewise, in the tax area, the fact that a significant number of hedge funds are established in offshore financial centers that are tax havens has focused attention on whether offshore hedge funds are associated with illegal tax avoidance and are taking advantage of their offshore situs for other inappropriate purposes.

- In the regulatory area, the U.S. regulatory agencies and the Treasury Department should continue to work with their counterparts internationally to consider measures to encourage offshore financial centers to adopt and comply with internationally-agreed upon standards developed by international organizations of regulators or supervisory authorities. A variety of incentives could be used:

  – A higher risk weight could be imposed on counterparty transactions for banks doing business with a financial entity operating out of an offshore jurisdiction that does not comply with Basle Core Principles.

  – Offshore financial centers' ability to join Basle-sponsored working groups and IOSCO could be made contingent on progress towards implementation of international supervisory and regulatory standards.

  – The G-7 and other countries with close relations with financial centers could press these centers to comply with international norms.

- In the tax area, the prevalence of hedge funds in offshore financial centers raises a number of tax policy and other issues. These issues, however, as well as issues raised by LTCM events related to the tax treatment of total return equity swaps, are beyond the scope of this report and are being addressed separately by Treasury.

8. Additional Potential Steps

Through its constituent agencies, the Working Group will be monitoring the credit risk management policies of large commercial and investment banks and assessing the effectiveness of the measures outlined above as a means of addressing concerns about excessive leverage on the part of hedge funds and other highly leveraged market participants. Although the Working Group is not making additional recommendations at this time, if further evidence emerges that indirect regulation of currently unregulated market participants is not working effectively to constrain leverage, there are several matters that could be given further consideration to address concerns about leverage.

- Consolidated supervision of broker-dealers and their currently unregulated affiliates, including enterprise-wide capital standards. This would enhance the current regulatory regime applicable to investment banking firms. Affiliates of broker-dealers are often large, generally highly leveraged, and are growing in significance. Problems at an unregulated affiliate can affect the regulated broker-dealer adversely and the trading activities of these affiliates can have systemic risk implications.

- Direct regulation of hedge funds. For highly leveraged hedge funds, regulatory restraints, such as capital requirements, could serve to constrain more effectively their degree of leverage and the probability of a failure with systemic implications. It is possible, however, that directly regulating these institutions could drive some of them offshore, which could make regulation less effective. In addition, direct regulation of hedge funds could present formidable challenges in terms of cost and effectiveness. Therefore, we believe that the measures discussed above would best address concerns related to systemic risk without the potential attendant costs of direct regulation of hedge funds.

- Direct regulation of derivatives dealers unaffiliated with a federally regulated entity. Capital and other requirements could help to reduce the degree of leverage in these financial institutions. Bringing unaffiliated derivatives dealers into the regulatory regime, together with hedge funds and the unregulated affiliates of broker-dealers, would expand the regulatory net to cover additional potential sources of systemic risk. There could be difficulties in implementation that might not be completely offset by the benefits, particularly if institutions were driven

42

offshore. In any event, these issues are being studied and considered in the context of the Working Group's upcoming study of over the counter derivatives.

Concerns have been expressed about the activities of highly leveraged institutions with respect to their impact on market dynamics generally and vulnerable economies in particular. Such activity can affect markets in some circumstances and for limited periods although, as a number of independent studies that have been undertaken so far have suggested, the activities of highly leveraged institutions do not appear to have played a significant role in precipitating the financial market crises of the past few years. Further study of this issue will be undertaken by the Financial Stability Forum, recently established by the G-7.

The increase in cross-border financial flows, however, highlights the importance of an appropriate financial regulatory structure. In particular, emerging market economies could consider implementing protections, as exist in many major market financial centers, to promote market integrity and reduce systemic vulnerability. The Working Group believes that it is important for the international financial institutions and international regulatory bodies to work closely with emerging market economies in the development of better institutional arrangements, standards, and practices in these areas.

APPENDICES

APPENDIX A

ADDITIONAL INFORMATION ON HEDGE FUNDS

1. Hedge Fund Performance Fees, Leverage, and Short-term Outlook

Hedge funds are distinct in several important ways from other types of investment vehicles. Whether domestic or offshore, hedge funds generally share three operational characteristics that set them apart from mutual funds, private pension funds, and bank personal trusts: (1) hedge funds charge advisory fees based on performance;[1] (2) they use leverage more aggressively; and (3) they pursue short-term investment strategies. The performance fees encourage risk taking while leverage and short-term strategies enable the funds to compound the risks they are willing to bear.

Performance fees. Performance-based fees represent a strong incentive for risk taking. A typical hedge fund will charge a fee amounting to 20 percent of the gains above a specified benchmark or watermark over a one-year period. In most cases, the benchmark is the fund's net asset value at the beginning of the measurement period.[2] Performance fees encourage investment strategies that emphasize the probability of exceeding the return threshold. These strategies invariably entail greater risk of loss. The investment stake that fund managers typically have in a fund, however, would tend to mitigate incentive for excessive risk taking.

Leverage. Leverage allows hedge funds to magnify their exposures and, as a direct consequence, magnify their risks. Hedge funds are limited in their use of leverage only by the willingness of their creditors and counterparties to provide it. The funds typically operate with a balance-sheet leverage of less than 2-to-1, but higher balance-sheet leverage is not uncommon.

In contrast, the Investment Company Act of 1940 denies mutual funds such a high degree of leverage by limiting their issuance of "senior securities."[3] In practice, a mutual fund's debt effectively may not exceed 33 1/3% of its total assets. For this purpose, certain trading practices,

---

[1] Some mutual fund advisers receive performance-based compensation based on "fulcrum fees." With a fulcrum fee, an adviser's compensation increases or decreases depending on how the fund performs relative to an appropriate index or other measure of performance over a specified period. See section 205(b)(2) of the Investment Advisers Act. In permitting mutual fund advisers to receive fulcrum fees, Congress noted that these types of fees "would insulate investment company shareholders from arrangements that give investment managers a direct pecuniary interest in pursuing high risk investment policies." H.R. Rep. No. 1382, 91st Cong., 2nd Sess. 41 (1970); S.Rep. No. 184, 91st Cong., 1st Sess. 45 (1969). Additionally, a mutual fund whose investors are limited to high-net worth persons and institutions may pay other types of performance-based compensation. See Investment Advisers Act rule 205-3. (17 CFR 275.205-3)

[2] In a small number of cases, the benchmark is the S&P 500.

[3] For purposes of the Act's asset coverage test, a senior security generally includes "any bond, debenture, note, or similar obligation or instrument constituting a security and evidencing indebtedness, and any stock of a class having priority over any other class as to distribution of assets or payment of dividends" (*i.e.*, preferred stock). 15 USC 80a-18(g). The term does not include certain loans made "for temporary purposes only and in an amount net exceeding 5 percent ... of the value of the total assets of the issuer at the time when the loan is made." A loan is presumed to be for temporary purposes if it is repaid within 60 days and is not extended or renewed. *Id.*

such as reverse repurchase agreements and short sales, may involve the issuance of a senior security under the Investment Company Act.[4] The SEC also requires that mutual funds limit their investments in illiquid assets to 15% of net assets (10% in the case of money market funds). This limits the ability of a mutual fund to invest in illiquid derivatives.[5]

Certain derivatives may not constitute "balance-sheet" leverage, but might represent "economic" leverage (*i.e.*, they display heightened price sensitivity to market fluctuations). The Investment Company Act does not contain broad prohibitions on a mutual fund's investment in any particular type of instruments, including derivatives. A mutual fund that is investing, or may invest, in derivatives that present risks must provide prospectus disclosure about these transactions and the risks involved. The SEC also has emphasized the importance of the role of mutual fund directors in the oversight of fund derivative investments, risk management, internal controls, and disclosure, in order to assure that mutual fund assets are properly valued.

Hedge funds obtain economic leverage in various ways, such as through the use of repurchase agreements, short positions, and derivative contracts. At times, the choice of investment is influenced by the availability of leverage. In recent years, for example, government bond markets around the globe have become attractive investment locations for hedge funds, in part because of the liquidity of these markets and in part because of related repo markets that allowed the funds to leverage their positions.

Short-term investment strategies. Hedge funds are generally not buy-and-hold investors. In the first place, performance fees make it important for the funds to show substantial gains within a year. More importantly, hedge funds tend to seek prices that either diverge from fundamentals or offer arbitrage opportunities. Since these circumstances are supposed to be temporary, the funds hope to make money and unwind their positions in a short period of time. The propensity of hedge funds to alter market positions quickly distinguishes them from pension funds and bank personal trusts. Mutual funds, however, are similar to hedge funds in that they can quickly liquidate portfolios, but because of cost, tax, and other considerations, they may be less likely to shift their market positions often.

---

[4] The SEC requires funds to "cover" obligations created through these techniques by establishing segregated accounts consisting of liquid assets in an amount at least equal in value to the obligations. See, for example, Investment Company Act Release No. 10666 (Apr. 18, 1979); Merrill Lynch Asset Management, L.P. (pub. avail. July 2, 1996). See also Appendix B of this report.

[5] An illiquid asset is any asset that may not be sold or disposed of in the ordinary course of business within seven days at approximately the value at which the mutual fund has valued the investment. See Investment Company Act Release No. 18612 (Mar. 12, 1992).

Figure 1: Annual Returns of Hedge Funds by Investment Style

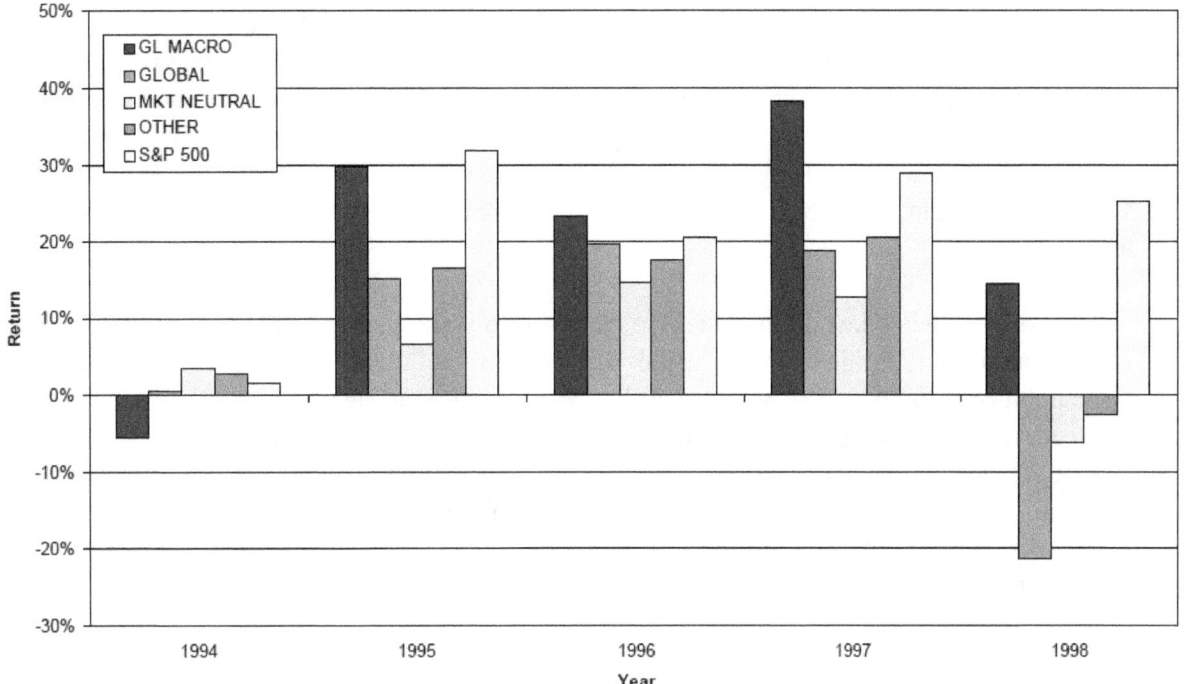

Estimates based on data provided by MAR/Hedge.

2. Hedge Fund Performance and Survival

In recent years, the performance of hedge funds has varied widely depending on the type of fund and the time period. Figure 1 compares the performance of four classes of hedge funds with the S&P 500 based on annual returns from 1994 to 1997. No class of funds consistently outperformed the S&P 500. Global macro funds, that is, those funds that take positions based on their forecasts of global macroeconomic developments, enjoyed good returns from 1995 to 1997, a period characterized by a bull market in U.S. stocks and bonds. Only in 1996 and 1997, however, did these funds do better than the S&P 500. The global funds, which focus on foreign stocks and bonds, also did well during the period shown, but only in 1996 did they outperform the stock market. The market neutral funds, which focus on relative price movements of similar assets, tended to perform relatively poorly, except in 1994 when most of the other funds seem to have suffered from the bear market in U.S. bonds and from the Mexican crisis at the end of that year.

The larger hedge funds — specifically the global macro funds and the global funds — are on the average riskier investments than the stock market as a whole. Table 1 below compares the average returns and risks among hedge fund categories and the U.S. stock market during the period from January 1994 to December 1997. During this period, global macro and global funds showed more impressive performance than the other hedge funds but they also took on greater risk. The average volatilities of these two classes of funds exceeded that of the stock market as a whole. The market-neutral funds and other funds performed poorly relative to S&P 500 but did so with less volatility than the stock market. The table also reports average Sharpe ratios, which measure returns relative to risk.[6] Based on these ratios, the S&P 500 represented a better trade-off of risk and return than the global macro and global funds but a worse trade-off than the other hedge funds.

The risks the funds take and their need to meet return watermarks tend to lead to high failure rates. The funds that fail, however, usually close before net asset values fall to zero. Table 2 shows the number of funds that survived over different periods starting from a sample of 397 funds in December 1994. For this entire sample of funds, fewer than three-fifths survived through the end of 1998.[7] The global macro funds, which are the funds with the highest returns, show the lowest survival rate with only slightly more than one-third of the funds still in operation after four years. The market neutral funds with the lowest return volatilities display the highest survival rate, with more than three-fourths of the funds surviving through June 1998.

Table 1
Sharpe Ratios and Average Monthly Returns
1994 -1998

Classification	Mean Return	Mean Volatility	Sharpe Ratio
Global Macro	0.212	0.179	1.318
Global	0.095	0.220	1.285
Market Neutral	0.068	0.062	4.309
Other	0.115	0.121	1.965
S&P 500	0.210	0.131	1.604

Estimates based on data provided by MAR/Hedge.

---

[6] There are different ways to define the Sharpe ratio. In this study, we derive the Sharpe ratios by dividing the mean of the monthly returns by the standard deviation, or volatility, for each individual fund. A higher Sharpe ratio implies a better risk-return tradeoff for a particular fund. Since all the numbers in Table 1 are averages of the statistics for individual funds, the average Sharpe ratio cannot be derived by taking the quotient of the other two columns.

[7] Brown, Goetzmann, and Ibbotson, 1997, estimate similar survival rates for their sample of offshore hedge funds and for a different sample period. See their paper, "Offshore Hedge Funds: Survival and Performance, 1989-1995," NBER Working Paper 5909.

Table 2
Survival of Hedge Funds
1994 -1998

	Global Macro	Global	Market Neutral	Other	Total
1994	91.2%	100%	98.7%	100%	98.5%
1995	68.4%	94.7%	93.6%	71.7%	85.4%
1996	57.9%	92.9%	87.2%	65.2%	80.4%
1997	42.1%	76.5%	79.5%	63.0%	67.0%
1998	35.1%	62.4%	64.1%	57.6%	57.7%

Estimates based on data provided by MAR/Hedge.

3. Market Impact, Positive and Negative

Providing liquidity to markets

Some hedge funds, as well as other market participants, undertake investment positions on the relative prices of related assets when the relative prices diverge from either historical norms or from the levels justified by fundamental macroeconomic considerations. These investors provide liquidity to markets because they buy and sell assets against prevailing market sentiment with the effect of mitigating temporary supply and demand imbalances. They buy the asset whose price has been driven down relative to the price of other related assets while selling the relatively overvalued asset.

Convergence or "arbitrage" trades are conducted in a variety of markets. One such market is the Treasury market where "arbitrage" trades smooth out price anomalies between similar Treasury securities issues.[8] This activity provides liquidity to other investors who benefit from the ability to buy or sell comparable Treasury securities at relatively uniform prices. Another convergence trade when corporate debt yields are unusually high relative to the yield on government debt is the bet that the credit spread will fall back to historical levels. In this investment, the investor buys corporate debt and sells government securities. Such trading can reduce the volatility in corporate debt spreads, reducing the riskiness in the timing of corporate debt issuance.

Normally, convergence traders smooth anomalous variations in the prices of related assets. On rare occasions, these traders may choose to or be forced to withdraw from the markets.

---

[8] In these trades, an investor constructs an estimated yield curve and buys Treasuries whose yield are above the curve while selling those whose yields are below the curve, on the conjecture that the anomalous yields will converge to the estimated yield curve. When this activity is conducted in sufficient volume, price anomalies quickly disappear.

When this occurs, the buying and selling pressures they otherwise would have absorbed or smoothed will immediately affect market prices. The market turmoil during late September and early October of 1998 was probably due, in part, to the withdrawal of convergence traders from the markets.

Reallocation of financial risk and economic activity

Hedge funds and other investors with high tolerance for risk play an important supporting role in a financial system in which various risks have been distributed across a broad spectrum of tradable financial instruments. With financial intermediation increasingly taking place in the capital markets instead of banking markets, prices play a larger role in the allocation of capital and risk. In this world, investors such as hedge funds that undertake a combination of long and short positions across markets help maintain the relative prices of related financial instruments.

Financial innovation over more than two decades has created a wide range of financial instruments with different types and degrees of risk. These instruments have unbundled the risks involved in financing real economic activity into distinct instruments that better match the preferences of investors. In doing so, they have most likely lowered the financing costs borne by the real sectors of the economy.

Alongside the innovation in financial instruments, specialization in the holding of risk has also emerged. Today's economy has moved away from the direct intermediation of credit where banks were the primary repositories of savers' wealth and channeled that capital to borrowers in the real sectors of the economy. In that traditional world, all risks, such as interest rate risk, liquidity risk, and credit risk were bundled together in bank deposits, bank loans, and the bank itself. Today's financial system is vastly different from that world. A larger proportion of financial risks are held directly by investors in the form of tradable securities, with banks and securities firms increasingly acting as originators, market makers, or underwriters of those securities, instead of as investors or lenders.

While financial risks are now placed directly in the hands of investors in the form of traded securities, those securities are highly differentiated. The appetite for risk among investors varies widely, and forcing all investors to hold identical risks would drive up the cost of financing real economic activity. Thus, competitive forces have created specialized financial instruments and investment vehicles with different risk profiles. A key underpinning of the creation of lower risk securities is the willingness of some investors to hold the financial instruments in which the remaining risks have been concentrated. The activities of hedge funds and investors with a high tolerance for risk should be seen in the context of this reallocation of financial risks.

One example of the risk taking that supports this reallocation can be found in the interest rate swap market. That market has allowed lenders and borrowers with different attitudes towards interest rate risk to transfer the interest rate risk in the borrowing relationship to a third party through an interest rate swap contract, thus allowing better financing terms for the borrower. The ability of the swaps market to perform this transfer of risk, however, depends on the stability of the link between the prices of interest rate derivatives and benchmark interest rates — for instance, the spread between interest rate swap rates and Treasury rates. This stability in turn depends on the willingness of speculators and arbitrageurs, such as hedge funds, to undertake convergence trades when swap spreads diverge from normal patterns.

Mortgage-backed securities provide another example of the role of specialization. Structured mortgage-backed securities have split apart the interest rate and prepayment risks embedded in residential mortgages and repackaged those risks into a collection of securities whose risks range from relatively low to extremely risky. By creating a highly risky security into which interest rate risk or prepayment risk has been concentrated, other less risky securities are created that provide a large share of the funding for the residential mortgage market. In the absence of investors who are willing to hold the risky tranches, mortgage originators would demand higher financing terms from borrowers because their ability to securitize mortgages would be impaired. Investors with high-risk appetites, such as hedge funds, are important participants in this reallocation of risk. If such investors were to disappear, mortgage interest rates would likely be higher.

Recent studies of the impact of speculators on currency market stability

Several recent empirical studies have looked at the impact of hedge funds on currency market dynamics to try to determine whether such investors can "move" these markets in directions favorable to themselves, either through their own actions or through the tendency of other market participants to follow their lead. The empirical results suggest that there is little evidence that they have done so in the episodes studied, although the data used to conduct these studies are limited.

An IMF Occasional Paper from May 1998 by Barry Eichengreen and others finds some evidence that hedge funds played a leading role in precipitating the ERM crisis in 1992 by acting as market leaders that other institutional investors followed, but that they did so in response to economic fundamentals.[9] In other episodes, notably the 1994 bond market turbulence, hedge funds as a group bet that interest rates would decline and lost substantial sums when they in fact rose. Studies of the role of hedge funds in the Mexican crisis in 1994-95 suggest that domestic residents, not international investors, played the leading role.

This study's analysis of the 1997 Asian crises indicates that hedge funds participated in the months before the crisis in the large increase in the carry trade (in which investors borrowed at low interest rates in major currencies and invested at higher interest rates in the East Asian countries) but that they were not the dominant players. As investors became worried about Thai

---

[9] Barry Eichengreen and Donald Mathieson (with B. Chadha, A. Jansen, L. Kodres, and S. Sharma), *Hedge Funds and Financial Market Dynamics*, Occasional Paper No. 166 (Washington D.C.: International Monetary Fund, May 1998).

economic fundamentals and began selling the baht forward, the hedge funds also participated, but the available data suggest that they were at the rear of the herd of investors rather than in the lead. In addition, in the view of market participants, the baht was the only Asian currency for which the hedge funds' collectively took significant short positions.

A study by Brown, Goetzmann, and Park, reaches similar conclusions.[10] They find that, although hedge funds have often followed similar strategies since 1993 that sometimes increased their combined positions to significant levels, global hedge funds did not "move" exchange rates. They look in detail at the 1997 plunge of the Malaysian ringgit, finding that neither current nor one-month-previous ringgit returns vs. the U.S. dollar over the crisis periods can be explained by hedge fund positions. More generally, they find that there have been periods when the hedge funds have had very large exposures to Asian currencies, both positive and negative, but find no relation between these positions and current, past, or future movements in exchange rates.

---

[10] Stephen J. Brown, William N. Goetzmann, and James M. Park, *Hedge Funds and the Asian Currency Crisis of 1997*, NBER Working Paper No. 6427 (February 1998).

APPENDIX B

THE SEC AND HEDGE FUNDS

GENERAL FRAMEWORK

1. Exemptions from Securities Laws

The term "hedge fund" is not defined or used in the federal securities laws, including those administered by the Securities and Exchange Commission ("SEC," or "Commission"). Over time, the term has come to be used to refer to a variety of pooled investment vehicles that are not registered under the federal securities laws as investment companies, broker-dealers, or public corporations.

Hedge funds are typically structured as limited partnerships, limited liability companies, or other vehicles that provide pass-through tax treatment of investor earnings. Hedge fund sponsors, some of which are registered as investment advisers under the federal securities laws, are responsible for managing the investments of the fund. As compensation, they typically receive a management or administrative fee based on the amount of the fund's assets, together with a share of the profits or some other allocation based on the fund's investment performance.

To maximize flexibility, hedge funds operating in the United States are structured so as to be exempt from regulation under the Investment Company Act of 1940 ("Investment Company Act"). Most hedge funds rely on the "private" investment company exclusions in Sections 3(c)(1) and 3(c)(7) of the Investment Company Act.[1] These exclusions exempt certain pooled investment vehicles from the definition of "investment company" and from substantive regulation under the Investment Company Act.

A fund relying on the Section 3(c)(1) exclusion ("Section 3(c)(1) Fund") must comply with two basic conditions. The Section 3(c)(1) Fund's securities (other than short-term paper) may not be beneficially owned by more than 100 persons.[2] In addition, the fund must not be making or proposing to make a public offering of its securities.[3] Certain Section 3(c)(1) Funds

---

[1] 15 USC 80a-3(c)(1), -3(c)(7).

[2] 15 USC 80a-3(c)(1). To prevent circumvention of the 100-investor limit, section 3(c)(1) requires, in some instances, that a fund seeking to rely on section 3(c)(1) look through certain companies that hold its voting securities and count the company's security holders as beneficial owners of the fund's securities. The look-through provision applies if the company owns 10% or more of the fund's voting securities and is either an investment company or a private fund. Securities of the Section 3(c)(1) Fund owned by "knowledgeable employees" of the Fund or its investment adviser do not count toward the 100 security holder limit. See rule 3c-5 under the Investment Company Act [17 CFR 270.3c-5].

[3] 15 USC 80a-3(c)(1). The limitation on public offerings has been interpreted to permit "transactions by an issuer not involving any public offering" under section 4(2) of the Securities Act of 1933 [15 USC 77d(2)]. See, e.g., Engelberger Partnerships (Dec. 7, 1981). A fund formed under the laws of a jurisdiction other than the United States may make a private offering in the United States only if after the private offering the foreign fund's securities are held by no more than 100 beneficial owners resident in the United States, or if all of the beneficial

B-1

may be structured as a "master-feeder" arrangement, in which several feeder funds invest all of their assets in a master Section 3(c)(1) Fund.[4] These arrangements may not be used to circumvent the requirements of the Investment Company Act.[5]

A fund relying on the Section 3(c)(7) exclusion ("Section 3(c)(7) Fund") may sell its securities only to those persons who are "qualified purchasers."[6] A "qualified purchaser" is (i) any natural person who owns not less than $5 million in investments (as defined by the Commission),[7] (ii) a family-owned company that owns not less than $5 million in investments,[8] (iii) certain trusts,[9] and (iv) any other person (*e.g.*, an institutional investor) that owns and invests

---

owners resident in the United States are "qualified purchasers" as discussed below. See Touche Remnant & Co. (Aug. 27, 1984) and note 6 *intra*. The foreign fund's private U.S. offering generally would be viewed as separate from the fund's simultaneous offshore public offering. See *id*. U.S. residents need not be counted toward these limits if they became owners as a result of activities beyond the control of the fund. See Investment Funds Institute of Canada (Mar. 4, 1996); Goodwin, Proctor & Hoar (Oct. 5, 1998).

[4] Fund sponsors may find it desirable, for tax or other reasons, to establish separate investment vehicles for U.S. investors and foreign investors, respectively. Rather than establishing two separate investment vehicles, the sponsor may establish an offshore master fund with domestic feeders (for U.S. investors) and offshore feeders (for foreign investors). Since all investment activities will be effected through the master fund rather than two separate funds, this structure may allow the sponsor to reduce the costs of operating side-by-side entities involving separate domestic and offshore investment vehicles .

[5] See *e.g.*, Cornish & Carey Commercial, Inc. (June 21, 1996).

[6] 15 USC 80a-3(c)(7). The securities of a Section 3(c)(7) Fund may also be owned by "knowledgeable employees" of the fund or its investment adviser, even if the employees do not fall within the definition of qualified purchaser. Rule 3c-5 under the Investment Company Act [17 CFR 370.3c-5]. In the case of a foreign fund relying on section 3(c)(7) to privately offer its securities in the United States, only beneficial owners resident in the United States must be qualified purchasers; the non-U.S. resident beneficial owners need not be qualified purchasers. See Goodwin, Proctor & Hoar (Feb. 28, 1997).

[7] Section 2(a)(51)(A)(i) of the Investment Company Act [15 USC 80a-2(a)(51)(A)(i)]. The term "investments" is defined in rule 2a51-1 under the Investment Company Act [17 CFR 270.2a51-1].

[8] A family company is a company "that is owned directly or indirectly by or for 2 or more natural persons who are related as siblings or spouse (including former spouses), or direct lineal descendants by birth or adoption, spouses of such persons, the estates of such persons, or foundations, charitable organizations, or trusts established by or for the benefit of such persons...." Section 2(a)(51)(A)(ii) of the Investment Company Act [15 USC 80a-2(a)(51)(A)(ii)].

[9] A trust may be a qualified purchaser if (i) it was not formed for the specific purpose of acquiring the securities offered, and (ii) the trustee or other person authorized to make decisions with respect to the trust, and each settlor or other person who has contributed assets to the trust, are qualified purchasers. Section 2(a)(51)(A)(iii) of the Investment Company Act [15 USC 80a-2(a)(51)(A)(iii)].

on a discretionary basis not less than $25 million in investments.[10] As is the case of a Section 3(c)(1) Fund, a Section 3(c)(7) Fund cannot make, or propose to make, a public offering of its securities.[11] Section 3(c)(7) was added to the Investment Company Act in 1996 as part of the National Securities Markets Improvement Act of 1996 ("NSMIA").[12]

Press reports suggest that Section 3(c)(7) Funds may have no more than 499 investors. While Section 3(c)(7) does not contain such a limitation, as a practical matter, Section 3(c)(7) Funds limit the number of record holders of their securities to less than 500 persons in order to avoid being subject to the public reporting requirements of the Securities Exchange Act of 1934 ("Securities Exchange Act").[13]

Private fund managers may be exempt from investment adviser registration under Section 203(b)(3) of the Investment Advisers Act of 1940 ("Investment Advisers Act"),[14] which exempts from registration any adviser who, during the preceding twelve months, had fewer than fifteen clients and who neither holds itself out generally to the public as an investment adviser, nor acts as an investment adviser to a registered investment company or business development company.[15] In computing the number of clients, a limited partnership counts as only one client of the general partner or any other person acting as investment adviser to the partnership.[16]

---

[10]   A qualified purchaser that meets the $25 million threshold may act for its own account or for the accounts of other qualified purchasers. Section 2(a)(51)(A)(iv) of the Investment Company Act [15 USC 80a-2(a)(51)(A)(iv)].

[11]   The public offering limitation appears to reflect Congress's concern that unsophisticated individuals not be inadvertently drawn into a Section 3(c)(7) Fund. *Privately Offered Investment Companies*, Investment Company Act Rel. No. 22597 (Apr. 3, 1997) [62 FR 17512 (Apr. 9, 1997)] at n.5.

[12]   P.L. No. 104-290 (1996) (codified in various sections of the United States Code).

[13]   See section 12(g) of the Securities Exchange Act of 1934 [15 USC 78l(g)].

[14]   15 USC 80b-203(b)(3)).

[15]   15 USC 80b-3(b).

[16]   17 CFR 275.203(b)(3)-1. The limited partnership must receive investment advice based on its investment objectives rather than the individual investment objectives of its limited partners. Rule 203(b)(3)-1 also contains a specific provision to address foreign investment advisers. The rule provides that an adviser with its principal office and place of business outside the United States must count only clients that are United States residents. An adviser with its principal office and place of business in the United States must count all clients, regardless of their place of residence. Thus, an off-shore investment adviser that manages more than fifteen hedge funds may rely on section 203(b)(3), provided that no more than fifteen of the funds are based in the United States and the other conditions of the exemption are met.

Typically, hedge funds also claim an exclusion from registration as broker-dealers under Section 15(a) of the Securities Exchange Act[17] based on the "trader" exception to the definition of "dealer." In general, a trader is an entity that trades securities solely for its own investment account and does not carry on a public securities business.[18] As defined by the Securities Exchange Act, a "dealer" buys and sells securities as part of a regular business.[19]

In addition, interests in hedge funds are sold privately to sophisticated, high net worth individuals to avoid registration of interests in the fund under the Securities Act of 1933 ("Securities Act"). Sales of interests in hedge funds typically are structured to take advantage of the "private offering" exemption under Section 4(2) of the Securities Act[20] or the related safe harbors under Regulation D thereunder.

2. Oversight of Broker-Dealer Exposure

Although the SEC generally does not regulate hedge funds, it does oversee broker-dealers that may act as creditors of, or counterparties to, these funds. Many hedge funds use prime brokers, which are also overseen by the SEC.[21]

The SEC relies on a number of regulatory tools, including capital, margin, and reporting requirements, in carrying out its oversight responsibilities. In addition, the SEC has examination authority and the ability to impose fines on those broker-dealers that violate the securities laws. SEC rules require broker-dealers to maintain a capital cushion to help them withstand the failure of a counterparty or periods of system-wide stress. For example, under the SEC's net capital rule, a broker-dealer must deduct from its net worth 100 percent of the value of all loans not fully

---

[17] 15 USC 78o(a).

[18] See, *e.g.,* Letter from Charles M. Horn, Division of Market Regulation, SEC, to David R. Burton, President, Burton Securities, dated December 5, 1977.

[19] 15 USC 78c(a)(5).

[20] 15 USC 77d(2). Section (4)(d) of the Securities Act provides that transactions by an issuer not involving any public offering are exempted from registration.

[21] Prime brokers are broker-dealers that clear and finance customer trades executed by one or more other broker-dealers, known as executing brokers. Prime brokers and executing brokers are required to register as broker-dealers under Section 15(a) of the Securities Exchange Act. A prime broker acts as a custodian for the customer's securities transactions and funds. Prime brokers also act as clearing facilities and accountants for all of a customer's securities transactions wherever executed. A prime broker for a hedge fund would, therefore, be expected to have greater knowledge as to the credit exposure posed by that hedge fund than would any executing broker.

collateralized by liquid securities.[22] In this way, the net capital rule helps to insulate broker-dealers from credit risk posed by counterparties, such as hedge funds.

Federal and self-regulatory organization ("SRO") margin rules also help protect against losses resulting from customer defaults by requiring customers (such as hedge funds) to provide collateral in amounts that depend on the market risk of the particular position.[23] Margin requirements imposed on broker-dealers help to maintain the safety and soundness of the individual firms. Such prudential measures also may have indirect benefits for the financial system as a whole.

As discussed further below, major U.S. securities firms also have controls in place to manage the credit risk posed by hedge funds and their customers. These controls generally include credit functions, such as the capability to perform credit analysis, approve and set counterparty credit limits, approve specific transactions, establish credit reserves, and manage overall credit exposure. A typical control would be a requirement that a firm's senior management approve transactions involving extensions of credit above authorized levels. In addition, information systems at some major firms enable risk managers to compute each firm's aggregate credit exposure by counterparty or product type and to monitor concentrations of counterparty risk.

The SEC staff also monitors the financial activities of material affiliates of certain large broker-dealers on a regular and continuous basis. Specifically, the risk assessment rules under the Securities Exchange Act[24] establish recordkeeping and reporting requirements for subject broker-dealers and their affiliates whose business activities are reasonably likely to have a material impact on the financial and operational conditions of the broker-dealer. These affiliates are known as "Material Associated Persons."[25]

The risk assessment rules require broker-dealers to maintain and file, on a quarterly basis, information concerning the financial activities of their Material Associated Persons. This information includes a description of a broker-dealer's policies for monitoring and controlling

---

[22] 17 CFR 240.15c3-1.

[23] Federal margin rules are administered by the Federal Reserve Board under Section 7 of the Securities Exchange Act. These rules are enforced by the SEC. SROs, including the securities exchanges and the National Association of Securities Dealers, which are overseen by the SEC, also impose margin requirements on their members.

[24] Rules 17h-1T and 17h-2T.

[25] The SEC adopted the rules pursuant to the authority granted by the Market Reform Act of 1990 ("Market Reform Act"). The Market Reform Act authorized the SEC to monitor and obtain information concerning the activities of significant affiliates of registered broker-dealers. The rules apply to broker-dealers that clear or carry customer accounts or have capital in excess of $20 million.

financial and operational risks to itself based on the activities of its Material Associated Persons. It also includes consolidated and consolidating financial statements for the ultimate holding company, and, as to each Material Associated Person, aggregate securities and commodities positions. Broker-dealers also must provide information concerning financial instruments with off-balance-sheet risk and the aggregate amount of bridge loans or other similar extensions of credit by each Material Associated Person.

With respect to instruments with off-balance-sheet risk, broker-dealers must furnish a counterparty breakdown where credit risk exceeds $100 million or 10% of tentative net capital (*i.e.*, capital before securities positions are adjusted to account for potential market movements), whichever is greater. For large securities firms, this threshold generally would not be met until counterparty concentration reaches between $200 million and $400 million. The SEC's risk assessment program has been in effect since December 1992. Currently, about 225 broker-dealers file information with the SEC pursuant to the risk assessment rules. To date, no hedge fund has triggered the reporting requirements under the credit risk concentration provisions.

Finally, under the Derivatives Policy Group ("DPG") framework, discussed in detail in Appendix F, the SEC collects additional risk assessment data on credit and market risk related to the OTC derivatives activities of five of the largest U.S. securities firms. The DPG framework, which is a voluntary framework, was developed by the six largest U.S. derivatives dealers, in coordination with the SEC and the Commodity Futures Trading Commission. The framework is designed to assist the SEC in evaluating risks presented by the OTC derivatives activities of unregulated affiliates of registered broker-dealers.

Specifically, the framework defines the responsibilities of the firm's governing body, or board of directors, as well as the management's responsibilities for implementing an effective risk management program. Under the framework, the board of directors is responsible for establishing written guidelines addressing items such as: (1) the scope of authorized activities; (2) quantitative guidelines for managing the firm's overall risk exposure; (3) the scope and frequency of reporting by management on risk exposures; and (4) the significant structural elements of the firm's risk management systems.

Under the DPG framework, the SEC also receives quarterly information on credit and market risks from the largest U.S. securities firms conducting a business in derivatives activities. This information includes the firms' top twenty counterparty exposures; credit reporting information by credit rating, industry segment, and country; and the reporting of financial information about derivatives activities, including net revenues, notional principal, and current exposures. The DPG counterparty disclosures did not identify any hedge funds because the reporting securities firms had no material uncollateralized exposures to hedge funds as measured by current exposures.

Practices followed by investment banks in their dealings with hedge funds

Several large broker-dealers had exposures to LTCM. Although the sudden liquidation of these exposures could have affected their earnings, it would not have threatened the solvency of those institutions. None of the six largest securities firms experienced realized or unrealized losses from LTCM during the third quarter of 1998; and their current exposures to LTCM during August and September of 1998 were fully collateralized with highly liquid securities. Despite its losses, LTCM was able to meet every margin and collateral call on a timely basis.

Nevertheless, the LTCM situation demonstrated that improvements could be made to the firms' risk management procedures. The largest securities firms have a centralized management structure with written policies and procedures for conducting due diligence into the financial condition and reputation of all prospective credit clients, including hedge funds. As discussed below, most firms appear to have appropriately allocated the technology and staffing resources needed to effectively manage risk on a global basis, including senior management involvement and oversight. Nevertheless, firms could strengthen and improve their systems of internal controls and risk management. In isolated instances, the SEC found deficiencies in the content or implementation of written policies and procedures, centralization of control, extent of active management involvement, or methods used to aggregate potential exposures globally by counterparty.

Credit management structure and oversight. At most large broker-dealers, the firm's board of directors will authorize a credit management committee to determine credit risk management policies in accordance with the board's authorizing guidelines. Some firms have one or more committees between the firm's board of directors and the credit department. In these instances, there is typically a hierarchy among the committees, with the most senior committee directly responsible to the board of directors. Senior management is usually represented on each committee.

Credit risk management policies are implemented on a global basis and executed by the credit department, usually under the guidance of the credit committee. The department has the responsibility for day-to-day credit operations, including due diligence, assignment of credit ratings, credit approvals, credit extensions, and monitoring of credit overages. Counterparties and clients are generally assigned to credit analysts according to industry sector or product group. To assure independence of credit evaluations and decisions, the credit department is independent of the firm's business units that assume the credit risk.

Credit approval process. Before executing transactions through a firm, every counterparty is subjected to a lengthy credit approval process. Most firms make exceptions to allow affiliates of existing counterparties to begin trading on a trade-by-trade basis (*i.e.*, each individual transaction is approved by the credit department before execution) or under temporary credit lines until a formal credit review and approval is completed. Generally, the process begins with a due diligence review by the credit analyst and ends with final approval by designated committees. In isolated firms, the credit department is vested with the sole authority for credit decisions. Each counterparty receives a credit rating and a corresponding credit line based on an in-depth analysis of the unique attributes of the counterparty, as well as its relationship with the firm.

Role of the credit analyst. The credit analyst evaluates whether a given counterparty will be able to meet its obligations to the firm. The analyst formally reviews all new accounts and approves or rejects prospective accounts under the guidance of the credit committee or a management committee with similar oversight. The evaluation of a new client, including a hedge fund, typically will includes on-site visits to assess the fund's overall strategy and operation. Initial credit approvals and the assignment of ratings are largely dependent on a number of factors, such as: character of management, credit history, financial performance, permanence of capital and access to additional capital, liquidity, asset quality, business integrity, experience of fund management, sensitivity to risk, use of leverage, back office operations, and mark-to-market procedures. The analyst will try to evaluate the fund's risk exposure by determining the liquidity of positions held and the potential amount of leverage employed. The analyst will conduct a review of financial reports, and prepare a trend analysis, ratio analysis, and industry comparison to make an overall determination as to how the counterparty's exposures may affect the firm's current risk structure. Based upon the analyst's overall assessment of the hedge fund, the firm will negotiate its collateral requirements.

For existing accounts, the analyst will approve or reject requests for changes to assigned credit limits. The analyst will conduct a periodic review, usually no less than annually, of hedge fund counterparties, to identify any changes in creditworthiness warranted by current market conditions. The analyst will also monitor overlines (*i.e.*, temporarily authorized credit exposures in excess of credit limits) and overages (*i.e.*, credit exposures in excess of credit limits due to market movements), and evaluate credit limits for counterparties experiencing material changes. At most firms, the analyst must note all credit actions in the credit monitoring system, including a record of all derivative transaction approvals. The analyst is also responsible for updating internal monitoring systems, counterparty credit files, approved product limits, and aggregate credit exposure limits. Credit analysts typically are not permitted to approve various complex and high risk transactions without documenting or evidencing senior management approval.

Assignment of credit ratings for hedge funds. Each counterparty is reviewed in order to evaluate individual credit strengths and weaknesses. Credit quality ratings are generally assigned on a numerical scale ranging from one through ten, reflecting minimal credit risks to the highest level of credit risk. The counterparty's credit risk rating will establish the level of trading that may be conducted at the firm and the required level of collateral. Internal credit ratings are continually reviewed and adjusted throughout the year.

Although hedge funds are not rated by credit rating agencies, credit analysts use similar criteria to assess creditworthiness. Criteria include market size, capital structure and leverage, financial stability, profitability, management, operating efficiency, legal documentation, and access to financial resources. Because hedge funds typically do not provide as much disclosure as public reporting companies or registered entities, their ratings are inherently more subjective. Subjective factors such as the experience and track record of the hedge fund and the firm's past dealings and relationships with the hedge fund are significant factors in the rating. In contrast, the ratings for large, corporate counterparties are closely linked to publicly available financial statements and credit reports by credit rating agencies.

How credit limits are set and allocated for hedge funds. The assignment of credit limits is generally related to the assigned internal credit rating. Once an internal credit rating has been established, firms will determine the maximum amount of credit that may be extended across all products areas, along with limits on the term-to-maturity of transactions. At several firms, limits are set according to total counterparty risk across all products, as well as individual product lines. Limits are also set for all approved counterparties on a legal entity basis. In conjunction with the periodic review of the credit rating, firms issue a formal renewal of each counterparty's credit line.

Monitoring and surveillance. All major firms use a computerized credit system that is updated at the end of each day to determine current and potential exposures for credit transactions. These systems receive data feeds from various trading systems and information databases relating to counterparties, such as trade detail, daily mark-to-market detail, and collateral supporting potential credit exposure calculations. Various reports are generated to assist the credit analyst with daily maintenance of accounts, such as overage and excessive unsecured exposures.

Ability to assess current and potential exposure. In order to manage credit risk, most firms measure potential exposure ("PE") and current exposure ("CE") on a daily basis to evaluate the impact of potential changes in market conditions on the value of counterparty positions and collateral. As a practical matter, firms require collateral on current exposures based upon the creditworthiness of the counterparty and have systems to test for potential credit exposure which may trigger requests for additional collateral. Value-at-risk ("VaR") calculations are used to determine potential exposures by subjecting positions to market movements involving normal and abnormal movements in interest rates, foreign exchange rates, equity prices, and other market factors. Market models try to quantify the dollar amount a firm might lose (PE) if a counterparty were to default. These models estimate that credit losses will not exceed some set limit within a specified level of confidence, usually between 95% and 99%. Market models value trades under future economic conditions incorporating historic data to create scenarios. The models will reprice a portfolio and simulate possible future outcomes.

Most models do not incorporate all products traded by the firm. Firms initially included products they believed presented the highest risks to them, with the intent of including other credit sensitive products at some future date. Some firms do not have the ability to calculate and monitor aggregate exposure limits across all product lines in a VaR-based environment. For instance, some firms only include derivative and foreign exchange transactions, and not repurchase agreements, mortgage backed securities and forwards. A firm's inability to evaluate exposures across all product lines could considerably underestimate credit exposures during periods of extreme market volatility. These firms are currently considering implementing future enhancements to their credit-based systems to include calculations of potential exposures for every product.

Overages. Overages occur when counterparties exceed their assigned credit limit for potential unsecured exposures. Overages may occur due to new transactions that exceed the approved credit limits or, more commonly, due to market movements that affect existing positions. Firms will monitor and resolve overages in several different ways, including: raising the overall credit limit within certain guidelines, checking for system problems or input errors, reviewing for additional collateral not considered, restricting further trades, or requiring the counterparty to unwind or offset certain risks associated with the exposure. The credit analyst is responsible for finding and alerting the appropriate parties responsible for dealing with credit overages. Frequently, overages are resolved by evaluating current credit risk and increasing the credit limit.

To discourage internal violations of credit limits, firms may require an account executive to forfeit sales commissions on trades that prove to circumvent the firm's credit policies. For large or repeated violations, additional disciplinary consequences often include fines, censures, or other sanctions designed to enhance compliance with credit policies. Moreover, a written record of each credit policy violation may be produced and sent to the appropriate supervisor.

Risk mitigants. Firms use a number of tools to reduce counterparty risk, including netting and close out provisions, initial and maintenance margin requirements, and daily mark-to-market of positions with collateral posted by the counterparty.

Periodic reviews of hedge fund creditworthiness. The credit analyst is responsible for the daily monitoring of accounts as well as all periodic reviews. At most firms, credit committees also perform an oversight role. The committees are generally responsible for reviewing credit limits established for a fund at least once annually. These committees are guided by the analyst that oversees the fund on a daily basis.

Conclusion. The trading and credit losses incurred during the third quarter of 1998 highlighted certain weaknesses in firms' risk management control systems, senior management oversight, documentation, and compliance with internal policies.

For example, credit decisions to lend to hedge fund counterparties were not always consistent with the firm's overall credit standards. Prior to the market events of August 1998, many hedge fund counterparties provided limited or no information with respect to aggregate security portfolios, leverage, risk concentrations, performance, and trading strategies. Firms often did not impose collateral and financial disclosure requirements on hedge funds that reflected the greater risks of the hedge funds' activities. Credit decisions were often based upon qualitative assessments involving the reputation and prior performance history of hedge fund management.

Certain oversights may have compromised the credit process, including the setting of limits and margin requirements. Recognizing these deficiencies, many firms have begun to require enhanced disclosures from hedge fund counterparties in order to continue doing business.

In addition, while key qualitative components of effective risk management included risk-based measurements during periods of extreme market volatility, these measurements of potential exposure became virtually meaningless during the third quarter of 1998, as the volatility of the underlying securities increased beyond the historical levels incorporated into the risk models. Consequently, as statistical measurements of potential risk became less reliable, some firms shifted their emphasis to monitoring equity levels and increasing margin and collateral requirements for clients trading illiquid securities or experiencing financial difficulties.

Concentration and liquidity risks also may not have been appropriately factored into assumptions. Products that were not considered as risky, such as repurchase agreements and mortgage-backed securities, were not always factored into potential exposures. Permissible limits also may have been too large, given the concentration of such exposures.

Stress testing, an essential component of risk management, was not thoroughly performed at all firms. While most firms were stress testing their proprietary positions with parallel volatility curve shifts and correlations, aggregate counterparty credit exposures were not always routinely stress tested. Furthermore, believing that credit exposures were protected by collateral, some firms did not formally review or limit their exposure to market movements based on an analysis of aggregate firm and customer positions.

Most large firms have made changes and enhancements to their risk management processes in response to the market turmoil. In August 1998, the firms became very concerned with their exposure to LTCM and other hedge fund counterparties. Consequently, they immediately began evaluating their internal risk management systems and controls. Corrective actions to strengthen the current operating structure and reduce credit exposures were considered or implemented. Firms are now more strictly adhering to stated policies, enhancing their back-testing and stress testing for high risk hedge fund portfolios, tightening their margin and collateral requirements, and updating their risk models to reflect recent market volatility. Moreover, several firms have created additional monitoring reports to document daily hedge fund exposures and weekly limit violations. Finally, as noted above, most firms are requiring more comprehensive financial disclosures from all hedge fund and other highly-leveraged institutional counterparties, and are reviewing their geographic and other concentrations.

The Commission will issue non-public inspection findings to several large broker-dealers addressing the strengths and weaknesses of their particular credit risk management structure, credit control procedures, and firms' implementation of credit policies.

3. Management of Clearing Risks

Section 17A of the Securities Exchange Act gives the Commission the authority to register and regulate clearing agencies. Clearing agencies registered with the Commission include the National Securities Clearing Corporation ("NSCC"), the Government Securities Clearing Corporation ("GSCC"), and the MBS Clearing Corporation ("MBSCC"), as well as the Depository Trust Company ("DTC"). These clearing agencies establish the rules governing the clearance and settlement of securities transactions, subject to the Commission's review and approval.

Generally, the rules of the clearing agencies do not provide for unregulated hedge funds to become direct clearing members.[26] Therefore, hedge funds must use clearing agency members (*i.e.*, banks and broker-dealers) for clearance and settlement of their transactions. As a result, the clearance and settlement system's exposure to hedge funds is no greater than its exposure to any other customer of a clearing broker-dealer or bank.

Clearance risk

After a trade is executed, clearing agencies are responsible for the transfer of securities and funds, and generally guarantee settlement. To guarantee settlement, clearing agencies interpose themselves between the counterparties and become the buyer to every seller and the seller to every buyer. As a result, clearing agencies incur certain risks, including counterparty/credit risk (*i.e.*, the possibility that a clearing member buyer or seller might default on its obligations) and market risk (*i.e.*, the possibility of financial loss caused by adverse movements in market price).

Clearing agencies mitigate these risks by employing risk management procedures, such as:

- **Establishing admission criteria**. Membership standards require every member to be creditworthy upon admission, and exclude entities that may increase risk.

- **Marking positions to market.** All unsettled securities or fail positions are marked to market and the clearing member failing to deliver the securities may be required to pay a mark-to-market adjustment depending on whether the price of the security rises or falls.

---

[26] There is no statutory prohibition against the admission of hedge funds as members of registered clearing agencies, but a clearing agency's rules would have to provide for the admission of hedge funds as members or participants. The Commission must approve clearing agency rules before they are implemented, but not the admission of individual participants. At least one clearing agency, MBSCC, has a hedge fund member (Long-Term Capital Portfolio, L.P., an affiliate of Long-Term Capital Partners). It is important to note that MBSCC does not guarantee trades like NSCC, or hold securities like DTC; therefore, MBSCC is not exposed to similar counterparty or market risks.

- **Monitoring current and potential exposures.** Clearing agencies routinely monitor members' creditworthiness through financial reporting requirements. The clearing agencies also coordinate their surveillance activities among each other, the exchanges, and the NASD.

- **Maintaining liquidity facilities** (clearing fund and lines of credit). Clearing members are required to contribute to a clearing fund, which is designed to mutualize the risk of a member's default. Clearing agencies also use lines of credit as a source of liquidity in the event of a member's default.

4. Other Issues Raised by LTCM

Issues concerning the size and organization of hedge funds

General issues. A wide variety of investment vehicles, other than hedge funds, rely on the exemptions from the Investment Company Act under Sections 3(c)(1) and 3(c)(7). These private funds include venture capital pools, asset securitization vehicles, family estate planning vehicles, and small groups of individual investors, such as investment clubs.

As noted above, Section 3(c)(1) Funds and Section 3(c)(7) Funds are not subject to the substantive protections of the Investment Company Act. These protections include limits on the extent to which an investment company can engage in leveraging. A closed-end investment company, for example, cannot issue a senior security unless, after giving effect to its issuance, the senior security will have asset coverage of at least 300% if the senior security is a debt security, or 200% if the senior security is preferred stock.[27] An open-end fund may not issue any senior securities, although it may borrow from a bank, subject to a 300% asset coverage test.[28]

Investors in private hedge funds typically are institutions and wealthy individuals that are in a position to appreciate and assume, or protect themselves from, the risks associated with hedge funds and other types of private investment pools. Although hedge funds may present certain risks, these vehicles generally have not been associated with traditional investor protection issues (such as self-dealing by the fund's manager). Investors in private funds typically receive disclosure concerning the risks presented by these funds. The antifraud provisions of the

---

[27] Section 18(a) of the Investment Company Act [15 USC 80a-18(a)].

[28] Section 18(f)(1) of the Investment Company Act [15 USC 80a-18(f)(1)]. The Division of Investment Management has taken the position that certain trading techniques, such as reverse repos and short sales, may involve the issuance of a senior security for purposes of the Act's leverage limitations. See, *e.g., Securities Trading Practices of Registered Investment Companies*, Investment Company Act Rel. No. 10666 (April 18, 1979) [45 FR 25128 (April 27, 1979)]; *Guidelines for the Preparation of Form N-8B-1*, Investment Company Act Rel. No. 7221 (June 9, 1972) [37 FR 12790 (June 24, 1972)].

Securities Act and the Securities Exchange Act also apply to the sale of a private fund's securities, whether or not the private fund is registered under the Investment Company Act.

As with other private funds, investors in private hedge funds may sustain losses commensurate with higher investment risks. Abuses by hedge fund sponsors are also possible. Congress has determined that hedge funds that rely on Sections 3(c)(1) and 3(c)(7) do not warrant Investment Company Act regulation, either because of the relatively small number of investors involved (in the case of Section 3(c)(1) Funds), or because the investors have sufficient investment experience to understand and bear the risks involved (in the case of Section 3(c)(7) Funds).[29]

Options for imposing additional restrictions on hedge funds. The imposition of additional limits on hedge funds that seek to rely on Sections 3(c)(1) or 3(c)(7), such as fund size limits, limits on the maximum amount that an investor may invest in a hedge fund, or limits on the number of investors in any one hedge fund, may not be an appropriate or effective means to address the perceived risks of hedge funds. First, a provision that seeks to impose additional limitations on hedge funds may also impose unwarranted burdens on other types of private investment pools, such as venture capital funds and structured financings, that may not raise the same concerns as hedge funds. For example, a limit on fund size or maximum individual investments could force a venture capital pool to reject or limit investment contributions. This could, in turn, limit investor opportunity and capital-raising efforts that benefit small and large businesses. Given the difficulties of formulating a precise definition of the term "hedge fund," drafting limitations that apply solely to hedge funds would be exceedingly difficult.

Similarly, reducing the 100 investor limitation in Section 3(c)(1), or introducing a limit on the number of investors in Section 3(c)(7), may not advance the investor protection concerns underlying the Investment Company Act.[30] Successful hedge fund sponsors, faced with limits on the number of investors, may be in a position to increase investment minimums (if any) and

---

[29] Section 3(c)(7) was premised on the notion that qualified purchasers are sufficiently sophisticated to appreciate the risks associated with investment pools that do not have the Investment Company Act's protections. The Securities Investment Promotion Act of 1996, S. Rep. No. 293, 104th Cong., 2d Sess. 10 (1996) (report of S. 1815, eventually enacted as the NSMIA). Section 3(c)(1) does not contain any provisions addressing the financial sophistication or wealth of investors in Section 3(c)(1) Funds. In order to take advantage of Section 4(2) of the Securities Act of 1933, however, hedge funds typically sell their securities to sophisticated, high net worth individuals.

[30] Decreasing the investor limit in section 3(c)(1) without introducing a similar limit into section 3(c)(7) could simply result in more hedge fund managers relying on section 3(c)(7). As noted above, private funds typically limit their investors to fewer than 500 in order to avoid the public reporting requirements of the Securities Exchange Act of 1934. It is unclear whether reducing the 500 record holder threshold would substantially reduce the size of hedge funds or result in more hedge funds filing reports with the Commission. Such a change would, however, subject many non-hedge fund issuers, particularly small businesses, to periodic reporting requirements that may not be appropriate under the circumstances.

maintain the amount of assets they have under management. Therefore, reducing the 100 investor limitation in Section 3(c)(1), or introducing a limit on the number of investors into Section 3(c)(7), may have little effect on the size of hedge funds. It could, however, have the unintended consequence of requiring similar adjustments to be made by other types of investment vehicles that are not ordinarily considered to be hedge funds.

Finally, precluding hedge funds from relying on Sections 3(c)(1) and 3(c)(7) would be conceptually at odds with the purpose of the Investment Company Act. The Act generally addresses structural protections, such as prohibitions against overreaching by insiders, and not an investment company's effects on the markets.

Issues concerning hedge fund managers

The manager of a hedge fund generally falls within the definition of investment adviser in Section 202(a)(1) of the Investment Advisers Act. In general, an investment adviser is any person who, for compensation, is in the business of advising others about investing in securities.[31] The Investment Advisers Act contains broad prohibitions against fraud. As a fiduciary, advisers owe their clients undivided loyalty, and may not engage in activity that conflicts with a client's interest without the client's informed consent. This duty requires advisers to make full disclosure to their clients of their business practices, fees, and conflicts of interest.[32]

The Advisers Act requires most advisers to register with the Commission if they have $25 million of assets under management unless an exemption from registration is available.[33] Registered advisers are subject to certain regulatory requirements designed to protect clients. For example, registered investment advisers are subject to books and records requirements,[34] cannot assign their advisory contracts without client consent,[35] cannot engage in principal transactions

---

[31] Certain persons, such as banks, are excepted from the definition of investment adviser.

[32] Rule 204-3 under the Investment Advisers Act [17 CFR 275.204-3].

[33] A investment adviser that manages less than $25 million of assets may not register with the Commission if the adviser is regulated in the State in which it maintains its principal office and place of business. Investment advisers registered with the Commission are not subject to state regulation. See generally sections 203 and 203A of the Investment Adviser Act [15 USC 80b-3, 80b-3A].

[34] Section 204 of the Investment Advisers Act [15 USC 80b-4].

[35] Section 205 of the Investment Advisers Act [15 USC 80b-5].

with their clients without prior client consent,[36] must take steps to protect client assets that are in their custody,[37] and are limited in the types of performance fees they can charge.[38]

As noted above, many hedge fund managers rely on the exemption from registration in Section 203(b)(3) and rule 203(b)(3)-1.[39] Advisers that do not register in reliance on Section 203(b)(3) remain subject to the antifraud provisions of Section 206 of the Investment Advisers Act.[40]

Modifying Section 203(b)(3) or rule 203(b)(3)-1 to limit or preclude hedge fund advisers from relying on them presents many of the same problems as discussed above with respect to Sections 3(c)(1) and 3(c)(7). Specifically, it would be difficult to limit any changes solely to hedge fund advisers. Moreover, requiring hedge fund managers to register as investment advisers would not seem to be an appropriate method to monitor hedge fund activity. Like the Investment Company Act's private fund exclusions, Section 203(b)(3) evidences a Congressional determination that clients of an adviser that has relatively few clients do not need the substantive protections of the Investment Advisers Act. These clients (particularly the sophisticated investors that typically invest in hedge funds) may be in a position to protect their own interests, either because of their size or their relationship to the investment adviser.

---

[36] Section 206 of the Investment Advisers Act [15 USC 80b-6].

[37] Rule 206(4)-2 under the Investment Advisers Act [17 CFR 275.206(4)-2].

[38] Recent amendments to the Advisers Act and the SEC's rules governing performance fees have increased the ability of registered investment advisers to charge performance fees and may have made registration more palatable to hedge fund advisers. For example, as a result of NSMIA, the performance fee restrictions do not apply to clients that are Section 3(c)(7) Funds. Advisers may also charge clients that are qualified purchasers performance fees without regard to the Advisers Act's performance fee prohibition. Investment Advisers Act rule 205-3.

[39] Some hedge fund managers register under the Investment Advisers Act because an exemption from registration is unavailable. A hedge fund manager may also choose to register if registration is important to its clients.

[40] Many investment advisers are also registered as broker-dealers.

APPENDIX C

THE CFTC AND HEDGE FUNDS

The term hedge fund is not defined under the Commodity Exchange Act ("CEA"). Thus no rule of the Commodity Futures Trading Commission ("CFTC") applies specifically to hedge funds as a separate category of regulated entity. However, to the extent that hedge funds trade commodity futures or option interests and have U.S. investors, their operators or advisors become subject to CFTC registration and/or reporting requirements. In addition, all persons, including hedge funds, who trade on U.S. commodity futures and commodity option exchanges are subject to reporting requirements with respect to large, open positions held on regulated markets as well as limits concerning speculative positions in certain contracts.

While these regulations may require the operators of the hedge funds to report to the CFTC information concerning hedge fund trading of on-exchange commodity futures and option contracts, they generally do not require reporting of information concerning the hedge funds' activities in other markets. Consequently, these requirements would not necessarily provide the CFTC with an "early warning" of any financial difficulty that may arise from trading activity.

1. Description of CPO and CTA Regulation

If hedge funds have U.S. investors and trade commodity futures contracts or commodity options, these funds would be commodity pools under the CEA. The CEA subjects the operators of commodity pools ("CPOs") and their advisors ("CTAs") — but not the pools themselves — to regulation.[1]

The regulatory scheme for CPOs and CTAs is designed to protect investors in commodity pools and customers of CTAs against fraud and overreaching. Thus, the CEA specifically forbids all CPOs and CTAs and their associated persons ("APs") from engaging in fraudulent transactions with pool participants and customers. In addition, the CEA sets forth general registration and other requirements for CPOs and CTAs that are designed to ensure the fitness of CPOs and CTAs; to protect commodity pool participants by ensuring that they are adequately informed about the material facts regarding the pool before they invest and during the course of their investment; and to protect customers of CTAs by ensuring that they receive adequate disclosures of information. To fulfill these statutory mandates, the CFTC has enacted registration, disclosure, reporting and recordkeeping requirements for CPOs and CTAs.[2] However, the CEA does not

---

[1] Part 30 of the CFTC's regulations requires CPOs and CTAs who operate and advise pools that trade on foreign exchanges and who have U.S. participants to register with the CFTC, or to obtain an exemption from registration, and to make certain disclosures. In addition, any CPO who is located in the U.S. is required to be registered as a CPO, even if it operates pools that have only non-U.S. investors.

[2] The CFTC has delegated to the National Futures Association ("NFA"), the futures industry self-regulatory organization, direct responsibility for the primary monitoring of compliance with those requirements. Thus, NFA, subject to CFTC oversight and review, receives and reviews applications for registration and grants, denies or conditionally registers CPOs and CTAs. In addition, NFA reviews the disclosure documents required to be provided by CPOs and CTAs to their customers and is responsible for conducting periodic inspections of registered persons.

impose minimum capital or other financial standards on CPOs and CTAs, nor does it impose restrictions on the financial interests that a commodity pool can trade.

CPO and CTA registration

Each person who comes within the statutory definition of the term "commodity pool operator"[3] or "commodity trading advisor"[4] must register with the CFTC, unless the person is excluded or exempt from registration pursuant to the CEA and CFTC regulations.[5] There are no general exceptions from registration that are comparable to those available to investment vehicles such as hedge funds under the federal securities laws. Consequently, a hedge fund that trades on commodity exchanges generally will be considered a commodity pool, its operator will be required to register as a CPO, and its commodity interest advisor will be required to register as a CTA.

Requirements applicable to CPOs and CTAs

Both the CEA and CFTC regulations prohibit CPOs and CTAs (regardless of registration status) from engaging in fraudulent practices with pool participants and customers. In addition, CFTC rules establish disclosure, reporting and recordkeeping requirements for each CPO and CTA "registered or required to be registered" under the CEA.

Each CPO who is registered or required to be registered and solicits prospective participants in a commodity pool must, absent an exemption, deliver to prospective participants, and file with the CFTC and NFA, a Disclosure Document containing specified information before the CPO may accept funds or other property in exchange for participation in the pool.[6] CTAs also must comply with disclosure requirements before they may enter into an agreement to direct or to guide a client's commodity interest trading account.[7]

---

[3] 7 USC § 1a(4).

[4] 7 USC § 1a(5)(A).

[5] CFTC Rules 4.5 and 4.6 exclude certain categories of person from the definitions of CPO and CTA. The exemptions from registration available to CPOs are found in CFTC Rule 4.13. The exemptions for CTAs are found in 7 USC §6m(1) and CFTC Rule 4.14. All persons required to be registered with the CFTC (except non-managed account CTAs) also must become members of NFA.

[6] CFTC Rules 4.21 and 4.24 through 4.26 set forth Disclosure Document requirements for CPOs.

[7] CFTC Rules 4.31 and 4.34 through 4.36 set forth Disclosure Document requirements for CTAs.

CPOs who are registered or required to be registered also must provide pool participants with financial statements concerning the pool's performance.[8] Specifically, the CPO must provide participants with an unaudited periodic Account Statement for the pool that contains Statements of Income (Loss) and Changes in Net Asset Value. The CPO also must provide participants with an audited Annual Report for the pool that contains the net asset value of the pool and Statements of Financial Condition, Income (Loss), Changes in Financial Position, and Changes in Ownership Equity.[9] Annual Reports are filed both with the CFTC and NFA, and while they provide an annual snapshot of the financial condition of a pool at a given point in time, they are not required to detail, and generally do not detail, the particular off-exchange activities or holdings of the pool.

CPOs and CTAs of hedge funds may qualify for exemptions from providing certain disclosures and reports to investors either because of the nature of their investors or to avoid duplicative or inconsistent regulation of funds operating primarily as securities trading vehicles. In addition, the CFTC has granted certain regulatory exemptions for CPOs of commodity pools that do not accept U.S. investors. Because these exemptions are not predicated on whether the pool at issue is a hedge fund, the CFTC does not have data to show how many hedge fund operators or advisors operate pursuant to one of the available exemptions. However, most, if not all, hedge fund operators or advisors who are registered as CPOs or CTAs likely operate pursuant to one of these reporting and recordkeeping exemptions.

The CFTC's Rule 4.12(b) provides relief from certain of the operational requirements applicable to registered CPOs who operate pools where the primary investment activity is in securities and the pool's commodity interest activity is limited and incidental to its securities trading.[10] To avail themselves of the foregoing relief, CPOs must file a written claim of exemption which identifies the CPO and the pool for which relief is being claimed and contains representations that the pool will be operated in accordance with the applicable criteria.

---

[8] Reporting requirements for registered CPOs are found in CFTC Rule 4.22.

[9] Registered CTAs are not subject to any financial reporting requirements to clients because their clients' funds must go directly into an account at a registered futures commission merchant ("FCM"). Therefore, unlike pool participants whose funds go into a pool for which a CPO subsequently opens an account with an FCM in the pool's name, CTA clients are provided with all relevant account information from the statements provided them by their FCMs.

[10] With respect to pools qualifying under Rule 4.12(b), CPOs may: (1) use an offering memorandum prepared in accordance with the Securities Act of 1933 ("'33 Act") or relevant exemption therefrom, supplemented by certain, but not all, Disclosure Document information otherwise required by CFTC rules to be included in the pool's Disclosure Document; (2) provide a quarterly statement that indicates the net asset value of the pool as of the end of the reporting period and the change in net asset value from the end of the previous reporting period in lieu of the prescribed Account Statement; (3) provide in lieu of the prescribed Annual Report a certified annual report which contains, at a minimum, Statements of Financial Condition and of Income (Loss); and (4) claim exemption from certain recordkeeping requirements.

Similar relief also is available to CPOs who operate pools whose only participants are persons who have substantial financial holdings and therefore are presumed to be sophisticated investors. The CFTC's Rule 4.7 provides relief from certain disclosure, reporting and recordkeeping requirements for registered CPOs who operate pools that are offered only to "qualified eligible participants" ("QEPs") and from disclosure and recordkeeping requirements for registered CTAs who advise only "qualified eligible clients" ("QECs"), as those terms are defined in the rule.[11] The relief available under Rule 4.7 is: (1) for CPOs and CTAs, an exemption from the requirement to provide a Disclosure Document, provided, however, that any offering memorandum or brochure distributed by the CPO or CTA must include all disclosures necessary to make the information contained therein not misleading; (2) for CPOs, permission to provide pool participants, in lieu of the prescribed Account Statement, a quarterly statement that indicates solely the net asset value of the pool as of the end of the reporting period, the change in net asset value from the end of the previous reporting period and the net asset value per unit; and (3) for CPOs, permission to provide pool participants and to file with the CFTC, in lieu of the prescribed certified Annual Report, an uncertified annual report containing, at a minimum, Statements of Financial Condition and of Income (Loss).[12]

To obtain relief under Rule 4.7, CPOs and CTAs must file a written claim of exemption. The claim must identify the CPO or CTA and must contain representations to the effect that the registrant qualifies for relief. In all likelihood, most hedge fund operators qualify for and obtain relief pursuant to Rule 4.7, since hedge fund investors usually meet the definition of QEP and because Rule 4.7 requires fewer affirmative disclosures by the CPO.

In addition to the above exemptions, the CFTC staff have granted exemptive relief from the disclosure, financial reporting and certain recordkeeping requirements to registered CPOs of offshore pools where: (1) the pool is organized and operated outside the U.S.; (2) none of the participants in the pool is a U.S. person; (3) no capital is committed, directly or indirectly, to the pool from U.S. sources; and (4) the CPO will not engage in any marketing activity with respect to

---

[11] QEPs and QECs fall within three general categories. The first category includes registered commodity and securities professionals, *e.g.*, futures commission merchants ("FCMs"), securities broker-dealers, the CPO and CTA of the pool at issue, and CPOs and CTAs who have been registered and active as such for the two prior years and who have $5,000,000 under management. The second category generally includes persons who are "accredited investors" as defined in Regulation D under the '33 Act and who meet a portfolio requirement of: (1) securities of unaffiliated issuers and other investments with an aggregate market value of $2,000,000; (2) $200,000 on deposit with an FCM in exchange-specified initial margin and option premiums for commodity interest transactions; or (3) a combination of (1) and (2). The third category includes entities in which all unit owners or participants are QEPs. In addition, non-U.S. persons, as defined in the rule, are QEPs. Because of the differences on limitation of loss typically existing between participating in a commodity pool and directly trading through a managed account, non-U.S. persons are not also QECs.

[12] Although Rule 4.7 provides an exemption from certain recordkeeping requirements, exempt CPOs still must maintain certain records in accordance with Rule 1.31; required books and records must be kept for five years from the date of making and must be readily accessible during the first two years.

U.S. persons. To avail themselves of this relief, CPOs must file a written claim of exemption. However, as is the case with Rule 4.7 and 4.12(b) exemptions, the CPO is not required to state whether the pool is a hedge fund.

Antifraud provisions

Regardless of their registration status, CPOs and CTAs are subject to the general antifraud provisions of the CEA and CFTC regulations, as well as specific prohibitions against fraud by CPOs and CTAs.[13] In addition, the CFTC has enacted rules that prohibit CPOs from accepting pool subscriptions in their own name and from commingling pool property with the property of any other person and that prohibit CTAs from accepting client property in the CTA's own name for the purpose of trading commodity interests.[14] CFTC rules also prohibit false and deceptive advertising.[15] These requirements, along with the registration and disclosure requirements, are designed to protect investors against fraud and overreaching by CPOs and CTAs.

2. Reporting of Exchange-Traded Commodity Positions

The CEA provides authority for the CFTC to enact appropriate regulations and to monitor trading activities of all traders on U.S. futures and commodity option exchanges. CFTC surveillance tools include speculative position limits and regulations that require daily position reporting for traders with large open positions in exchange-traded contracts. Since many hedge funds are also large traders who fall within these reporting requirements, the CFTC is able to monitor large on-exchange commodity interest trading on a daily basis. The CFTC's market surveillance mechanisms apply only to U.S. exchange-traded futures and commodity option contracts and not to other types of instruments and contracts. Since the exchange-traded positions held by hedge funds are often small compared to their positions in other markets, the CFTC's market surveillance systems cannot alone identify troubled hedge funds or systemic risks arising from major hedge fund losses.

Speculative position limits and position accountability rules

The CFTC is authorized to set "limits on the amounts of trading which may be done or positions which may be held by any person" for the purpose of protecting the integrity of the

---

[13] 7 USC § 4b prescribes antifraud activities for any person acting for or on behalf of any other person in connection with a contract of sale of any commodity in interstate commerce, made or to be made on or subject to the rules of a contract market or in connection with a futures contract. 7 USC § 4(o) specifically prohibits fraudulent transactions by CPOs and CTAs. In addition, CFTC Rules 32.9 and 33.10 prohibit fraud by any person in connection with commodity option transactions.

[14] CFTC Rules 4.20 and 4.30, respectively.

[15] CFTC Rules 4.41(a) and (b).

markets.[16] Thus, the CFTC, as well as the commodity exchanges, imposes speculative position limits to prevent market distortions.[17] To the extent that they trade on U.S. futures and commodity option exchanges, hedge funds and their operators and advisors are subject to these limits.

Hedging, and in some cases arbitrage, transactions are exempt from the CFTC's speculative position limits.[18] Hedge funds also may be able to obtain an exemption from the exchanges' speculative position limits for hedging or arbitrage transactions. In addition, in certain contract markets, such as those for U.S. Treasury bonds, foreign currencies and precious metals, speculative position limits have been replaced by position accountability rules.[19] Under these rules, traders can hold open positions in excess of exchange-established limits but must provide information regarding their positions on request.

Large-trader reporting system

It is unlawful for any person to hold a "reportable" futures position, *i.e.*, a position that equals or exceeds the quantities specified in CFTC rules, unless the person has filed reports of those positions in accordance with CFTC rules.[20] Under CFTC rules, each futures commission merchant ("FCM"), clearing member, and foreign broker must submit a report to the CFTC each business day with respect to each account for which there is a "reportable" position, except for accounts carried on the books of another FCM on a fully-disclosed basis.[21] Contract markets also must report to the CFTC each business day, by proprietary and customer account, on the positions that each clearing member is carrying.[22] Further, traders who hold a "reportable" position, are required to file upon call by the CFTC or its designee identifying information including: the name and address of the reporting trader; the principal business and occupation of the reporting trader; the name and address of each person whose commodity interest trading is

---

[16] 7 USC § 6a(a).

[17] The CFTC imposes speculative position limits solely on agricultural commodities. See CFTC Rule 150.2. In addition, under CFTC Rule 1.61, each commodity exchange (contract market) is required to establish speculative position limits, subject to CFTC approval (or exemption), for those contracts not specified in CFTC Rule 150.2.

[18] CFTC Rule 150.3.

[19] See 51 Fed. Reg. 51867 (October 15, 1991).

[20] 7 USC § 6i.

[21] CFTC Rule 17.00. The exact level of a reportable position differs from contract to contract and is defined in CFTC Rule 15.03.

[22] CFTC Rule 16.00.

controlled by the reporting trader; the name and address of each person who controls the trading of the reporting trader; and the names and locations of persons who guarantee the commodity interest trading accounts or who have a financial interest of ten percent or more in the reporting trader or accounts of the reporting trader.[23] Given their size, many hedge funds and their operators and advisors hold reportable market positions and therefore supply the CFTC with information about their commodity interest trading on U.S. exchanges. The CFTC has the power to inspect an entity's books and records to examine the complete details concerning all such transactions, positions, inventories, and commitments, including the names and addresses of all persons having any interest therein.[24] In addition, CFTC rules provide for special calls for information from traders and FCMs.[25]

3. Oversight of FCM Exposure to Hedge Funds

FCMs solicit and/or accept orders for the purchase or sale of futures and commodity options and accept funds (or extend credit in lieu thereof) to margin, guarantee or secure commodity interest transactions. FCMs can have financial exposures to hedge funds either because the hedge funds are customers of the FCM or because the FCM acts as a counterparty to the hedge fund in an OTC transaction. There are no special rules imposed on FCMs to limit their exposure to hedge funds or otherwise to restrict their dealings with hedge funds. However, the various protections that are designed to ensure the financial integrity of FCMs apply equally to all customer accounts carried by FCMs, whether such accounts are for trading by hedge funds or individual retail customers. In addition, any OTC activity undertaken by an FCM will be limited by the CFTC's minimum capital requirements for FCMs, which in general require FCMs to take a substantial charge to regulatory capital with respect to OTC derivative transactions.

Because of the role of FCMs in handling customer funds, they are subject to the most extensive financial requirements of any registrants under the CEA. The most important of these financial safeguards are as follows.

Margin

Customer margin requirements are designed to assure performance by the customer of its obligations under the futures contracts. The commodity exchanges set a minimum amount of

---

[23] CFTC Rule 18.04. The CFTC has recently proposed amending Form 40, the form on which this information is filed, in a manner that would divide the current reporting category of "Investment Groups" into distinct, more descriptive subcategories. The proposed subcategories include one for hedge funds. See *Changes in Reporting Levels for Large Trader Reports,* 64 Fed. Reg. 5200, 5203-04 (February 3, 1999) (Proposed Amendments to 17 CFR Parts 15 and 17).

[24] 7 USC § 6i; Rule 18.05.

[25] Rule 18.05 and Part 21 of the CFTC's rules.

margin that its member FCMs must receive from their customers in order to establish and to carry positions for these customers. The deposit the customer makes to establish its position is called "initial" margin. FCMs have the discretion to require their customers to provide funds in excess of the minimum margin requirements set by the exchange. Whether an FCM will exercise this discretion depends upon its assessment of a customer's creditworthiness. In normal market conditions, most FCMs would only charge sophisticated institutional customers such as hedge funds the exchange-set minimum initial margin.

Whenever losses in a customer's account erode the net equity in the account to maintenance margin levels set by the exchange (generally 70-75 percent of the initial margin level), the FCM will issue a "maintenance" margin call to the customer requiring the deposit of sufficient additional funds or collateral to bring the level of margin on deposit with the FCM up to 100 percent of the initial margin deposit. If market conditions change abruptly, an FCM can require additional margin deposits from a customer in as little as one hour's time.

Segregation of customer funds

The CEA and CFTC rules require FCMs to account separately for customer funds deposited to margin, guarantee or secure futures positions, and the accruals (gains or losses) on such positions, on their books and records.[26] All such customer funds must be segregated from the FCM's own funds and must be treated as belonging to the customer. An FCM may, however, pool all customer funds in a single account, as long as the account is clearly identified as belonging to customers. An FCM must always maintain in the segregated account, free from claims, sufficient funds to meet all the obligations it would owe to customers if their accounts were closed out at current market prices. Segregation also facilitates the transfer of accounts from a failing firm to a solvent one, allowing customers to maintain their positions without any disruption to the customer. Thus, segregation serves to protect the customer.

Minimum financial requirements

The CFTC prescribes both minimum financial requirements for FCMs and the standards for calculating how those requirements are met. The basic minimum adjusted net capital requirement for an FCM is the greater of (1) $250,000 or (2) four percent of customer segregated funds (less the market value of long options in customer accounts). The basic calculation that an FCM must make in order to demonstrate compliance with the minimum adjusted net capital requirement is as follows: current assets *minus* liabilities *minus* capital charges *equals* adjusted net capital.

FCM capital is a backup to margin and must be highly liquid so that an FCM can readily satisfy segregation requirements and obligations to all its customers should a particular customer

---

[26] See CEA Section 4d(2), 7 USC § 6d(2), and CFTC Rules 1.20-1.30, 1.32 and 1.36.

default.[27] CFTC rules are more restrictive than generally accepted accounting principles with respect to items such as receivables and prepaid expenses. Unsecured receivables, except in very limited circumstances, have essentially no value as regulatory capital. As a consequence, even though it may be permissible for an FCM to engage in certain OTC derivative transactions, the capital rules result in significant charges against regulatory capital with respect to OTC derivative transactions, and it is common practice for such transactions to be conducted through unregistered affiliates of the FCM.

Financial recordkeeping and reporting requirements

FCMs must prepare and keep current ledgers showing each transaction affecting their asset, liability, income, expense and capital accounts. An FCM must make and retain as a record open to inspection a formal computation of its adjusted net capital and minimum financial requirements as of the end of each month. Although these computations are only required monthly, an FCM should be able to demonstrate compliance with minimum financial requirements at all times. FCMs also must file financial reports on a quarterly basis[28] and submit reports certified by an independent public accountant as of the fiscal year end. (An applicant for registration as an FCM must also file a certified financial report.) If any material inadequacies in an FCM's internal controls are found by the independent public accountant, they must be reported.[29]

Risk assessment rules

As noted above, it is not uncommon for an unregistered affiliate of an FCM to engage in OTC derivative transactions. The CFTC, recognizing that these and other transactions conducted through unregulated affiliates of holding company systems that include FCMs can create risk for the regulated FCM, adopted rules that require FCMs that are part of holding company systems to file: (1) an organizational chart depicting the various entities with which the FCM is affiliated and identifying those entities that are "material affiliated persons;" (2) the FCM's policies, procedures and systems to manage the risks to the FCM's financial condition or operations arising from the activities of its affiliates; and (3) annual consolidated and consolidating financial statements.[30] The

---

[27] The CEA and CFTC rules prohibit the use of one customer's funds to satisfy obligations of another customer, so if there is a customer default on a margin call, an FCM may be required to put its own funds in the segregated account. See CEA Section 4d(2); CFTC Rule 1.23.

[28] The CFTC's financial reporting form for FCMs is Form 1-FR. Firms dually registered as FCMs and as securities broker-dealers can file a copy of the SEC FOCUS Report in lieu of Form 1-FR.

[29] See CFTC Rule 1.16(c), (d) and (e); CFTC Rule 1.12(d).

[30] CFTC Rule 1.15.

CFTC can also request additional information as conditions warrant, as it did following the recent difficulties experienced by LTCM.

4. Management of Clearance Risks

To the extent that hedge funds engage in commodity futures or options transactions on U.S. exchanges, they receive the benefits of the exchange clearing systems. The clearance and settlement system for each U.S. commodity futures or options exchange plays a key role in managing and containing risk in those markets and is essential to their efficiency and integrity. Although the rules of each exchange's clearinghouse differ, the clearinghouse for each exchange performs essentially the same function — it decreases credit risk by becoming the counterparty to, and guarantor of, every trade. The CFTC oversees the clearing systems for U.S. commodity futures and options exchanges.[31] The key elements of this clearinghouse system are as follows.[32]

Clearinghouse membership

Not all exchange members qualify for membership in the clearinghouse because the financial requirements for membership in a clearinghouse are more stringent than for membership in the exchange. Clearing members are monitored regularly to assure the members' continued compliance with applicable net capital requirements and to detect any financial problems before they affect the members' ability to meet their obligations. In addition, most clearinghouses require their members to contribute to the general clearinghouse guaranty fund. Each member's deposit is available to the clearinghouse to cover a default by that member and, if necessary, to cover a default by another clearing member.

Margin requirements

When a clearing member adds positions to its customer or proprietary accounts, it must deposit money, known as "original margin," to secure its obligations to the clearinghouse. The exchange or the clearinghouse sets the minimum amount of original margin that must be maintained to secure open positions.[33] In addition, open positions are "marked-to-market" daily; and the clearinghouse will debit or credit a member's account based on the changes in value of the

---

[31] For example, the Commodity Exchange Act and the CFTC regulations require any board of trade which has been designated as a contract market to submit to the CFTC for review all proposed rules, including those of the exchange's clearinghouse. 7 USC § 5a(8) and 5a(12); CFTC Rule 1.41.

[32] A comprehensive discussion of the clearance and settlement procedures of U.S. commodity exchanges can be found in Timothy Snider, Regulation of the Commodities Futures and Options Markets § 2.01-2.12 (2d ed. 1995).

[33] The amount of original margin that members are required to deposit is usually uniform. Most clearinghouses have authority to require higher levels of margin, sometimes referred to as "supermargin requirements," for particular clearing members in extraordinary circumstances.

member's open positions.[34] All members of a clearing organization are required to maintain accounts for the payment and collection of variation margin with at least one of the exchange's designated settlement banks.

Clearinghouse guarantee

When a trade takes place on the exchange floor, each trader must report it to the clearinghouse, where the trade is registered on the account of the trader's clearing firm. The clearinghouse then verifies the trade by matching the information from the buyer and the seller in order to clear the contract. Once the clearinghouse verifies and clears the contract, the clearinghouse is substituted for the original parties to the contract, becoming the "buyer to every seller" and the "seller to every buyer." Since the clearinghouse, as the "universal counterparty" to every cleared contract, guarantees performance of that contract, the parties to a trade do not need to know the identity of a counterparty prior to executing a trade, and need not be concerned about the creditworthiness of the original counterparty. In guaranteeing the payment of variation margin to clearing members with net gains on positions in their accounts, the clearinghouse substantially protects customers from the risks of a default by another customer or by a clearing member.

In the event of a customer default, the margin deposits made by the customer assist a clearing member in meeting its obligations to the clearinghouse. However, if a customer defaults on its margin payment to the clearing member and the member is unable to close out the customer's position before the equity in the account is exhausted, the clearing member must use its own funds to pay the variation margin owed to the clearinghouse and pay any additional variation margin required to cover losses sustained in closing out the position. This guarantee of payment by the clearing member provides market participants with substantial protection against defaults by other participants.

In the event of a default by a clearing member, the clearinghouse generally will be allowed, under its rules, to close out or transfer to other members all of the positions carried by the defaulting member. If obligations to the clearinghouse remain, the clearinghouse may use original margin deposited by the defaulting member to cover these obligations. The clearinghouse cannot use margin deposited on a defaulting member's customer positions to satisfy obligations other than those related to the defaulting member's customer accounts.[35] The clearinghouse has priority

---

[34] To the extent that the value of a member's account has increased above required minimum original margin levels, the member may withdraw any excess margin. By contrast, if the value of a member's account has fallen below required original margin levels, the member will be required to pay additional margin.

[35] Thus, a clearinghouse cannot use original margin funds deposited in connection with positions held by a defaulting member's customers to cover any obligations arising from the defaulting member's proprietary trading. However, the defaulting member's customers could be exposed to losses because of shortfalls in other customers' margin payments. This risk occurs because at the clearinghouse level customer funds are held in a single omnibus

with regard to original margin funds because those deposits constitute security to satisfy demands for variation margin owed on open positions. If a deficit still remains after the margin funds have been exhausted, then the clearinghouse can access the defaulting member's guaranty funds and will have recourse to its other assets, as well. If these funds still do not cover the deficit, most clearinghouses will assess their other clearing members to cover the balance.

5. LTCM and U.S. Futures Markets

The FCMs carrying U.S. exchange-traded futures and option positions for LTCM made timely margin calls related to those positions, and LTCM satisfied them. Even when conditions at LTCM came to a head in late September 1998 and there was a margin call made for tens of millions of dollars, LTCM's account equity was more than three times the size of the call so that even if LTCM had defaulted, futures market positions could have been liquidated without causing an impact on the financial conditions of the carrying FCMs. Even if events had further deteriorated so that LTCM ended up in a debit or deficit condition that it was unable to cover, the FCMs in question had substantial excess adjusted net capital with which to absorb a default. Nor were LTCM's exchange positions of such magnitude that a default by it likely would have caused significant disruption of the U.S. exchange-traded futures markets.

6. CFTC Analysis of Hedge Fund Data

The CFTC receives information from CPOs concerning commodity pools, some of which are hedge funds.[36] In addition, the CFTC has authority to request and receive additional information under CFTC Regulations 1.31 and 4.23 from CPOs about the trading activities of the commodities pools that they operate. After learning of LTCM's financial difficulties in late September 1998, CFTC staff determined to gather additional information concerning the current financial status of certain large commodity pools. Accordingly, in early October CFTC staff issued a request for information to operators of selected pools.

The selection criteria were (a) pools with total assets over $250 million *or* (b) pools with total assets somewhat less than $250 million and leverage greater than 2½-to-1. Ninety-nine CPOs operated at least one pool that met these criteria. Because the CPOs were required to report on all pools that they operated, whether or not all the pools met the criteria, information

---

account and all funds in this account could be used to satisfy obligations to the clearinghouse arising from customer positions. Thus, funds of one customer could be used to satisfy the obligations of another customer if the clearing member is unable to meet those obligations.

[36] There are more than 1000 funds operated by CPOs registered with the CFTC. As discussed *supra*, these CPOs file with the CFTC an annual report for each pool. In addition, CPOs must maintain certain records and provide copies to the CFTC upon request.

was received on 370 pools.[37] The information obtained was as of September 30, 1998. CFTC staff auditors analyzed this information and, in a number of cases, asked follow-up questions. Pools were also grouped into families of related pools, based on CFTC staff's understandings of such relationships.[38]

Size

The ten largest families of pools as measured by total assets as of year-end 1997 ranged from $11 billion to $129 billion, with an average size of $34 billion. As of September 30, 1998, the ten largest families ranged in size from $15 billion to $122 billion, with an average size of $36 billion. At the end of each period measured, approximately forty families had total assets greater then $1 billion, and approximately fifty had total assets greater than $500 million.

The total assets of the ten largest individual pools as of year-end 1997 ranged from $9 billion to $129 billion. By comparison, as of September 30, 1998, the total assets of the ten largest pools ranged from $10 billion to $122 billion. As was the case with families, for both dates there was a significant difference in size between the largest pool and the others on the list, as indicated by average size. The average size of the ten largest individual pools both at year-end 1997 and as of September 1998 was approximately $28 billion in total assets.

At both year-end 1997 and September 1998, approximately another 45 pools had total assets exceeding $1 billion. A total of approximately 150 pools at year-end 1997 and 130 pools at September 1998 had total assets exceeding $100 million. Thus, most pools operated by CFTC registrants had total assets under $100 million.

Leverage

CFTC staff also analyzed funds based on balance-sheet leverage, defined (for ease of computation) as total assets divided by total equity. The following leverage analysis focuses on the larger funds (those with total assets greater than $500 million), given the greater likelihood that the failure of such a fund might have systemic effects. It is important to emphasize that these figures are based on accounting data and do not include analysis of open positions, market strategies, or value at risk. An entity might have high balance-sheet leverage but, because of the

---

[37] To avoid double-counting, data on feeder pools was excluded, leaving about 270 pools. A feeder pool is a pool that invests most of its money in another pool or pools. The pools that it invests in may be operated by the same CPO or by other CPOs. Feeder pools may be tiered.

[38] Thus, this summary is based on the following information: (1) 1997 year-end annual reports filed by CPOs and (2) responses to the request for information sent by the CFTC to selected pool operators during the first week of October 1998 and steps taken by staff to follow up on that request. All of the 1998 and some of the 1997 information is based on unaudited reports. Because CFTC Rules do not require certain funds to provide financial statements (other than net asset value information) on a basis more frequently than annually, some funds did not provide total asset information for 1998.

low volatility and effective hedging of its positions, represent a lesser risk than another entity with low balance-sheet leverage but highly volatile and/or unhedged positions.

As of year-end 1997, the ratio for the ten families with the highest degree of leverage (among those who reported total assets greater than $500 million) ranged from 12 to 71. As of September 30, 1998, the leverage ratio for the ten most highly leveraged of this class of families ranged from 7 to 32. In each case, approximately another ten families had leverage ratios in excess of 2.5.

As of year-end 1997, the ratio for the most leveraged individual pools with total assets exceeding $500 million ranged from 27 to 67.[39] As of September 30, the ratio for the ten most leveraged pools ranged from 16 to 37. At year-end, there were three pools with leverage ratios in the forties, two pools with ratios in the thirties, and two with ratios in the twenties. The September figures reveal four pools with ratios in the thirties, two with ratios in the twenties, and two with ratios in the teens. Most funds operated by CFTC registrants had leverage of less than 2-to-1.

Creditors and counterparties

In the October request, the CFTC asked responding pools to list their five largest creditors and their five largest counterparties. The pools were not asked to identify the dollar amounts of the obligations. In analyzing the responses, CFTC staff noted that there were inconsistencies among the reporting firms as to who was classified as a creditor and who was classified as a counterparty. Accordingly, the data were analyzed to identify all instances where an entity was listed in either category. Eighty-six entities were listed at least once. The ten most frequently listed firms were all well-known banks, investment banks, or broker-dealers. Only four pools were mentioned at all as creditors or counterparties. None was in the top 35.[40]

Futures positions on U.S. exchanges

CFTC staff review large trader reports on a daily basis. After learning of LTCM's financial difficulties, the CFTC staff contacted FCMs carrying large positions on behalf of pools and confirmed that daily margin obligations continued to be met on a timely basis. CFTC staff also have reviewed recent futures positions of the ten largest pools that responded to the request for information. As of December 15, 1998, there were 33 instances where these pools had

---

[39] Two outliers are excluded from this analysis.

[40] It should be emphasized that these figures do not represent the dollar level of exposure for these firms. Rather, they only represent the number of instances a firm was listed as a creditor or as a counterparty. Thus, a firm listed once as a creditor with a $10 million loan outstanding would have more financial exposure than a firm that was listed 9 times but with each exposure being $1.1 million or less.

reportable futures positions. In 31 of these cases, the net positions represented less than 1 percent of the total open interest in the contract.

Withdrawal polices

CFTC staff also analyzed the withdrawal policies of the largest commodity pools to determine whether there were indications of a risk of a "rush to the exits" on December 31. CFTC staff contacted some of the larger funds that do allow significant withdrawals as of the end of the year. The CFTC concluded that funds operated by CFTC-registered pool operators were unlikely to experience significant liquidity problems in coping with redemptions at the end of 1998.

7. Conclusion

The CFTC and the exchanges have detailed information available on a daily basis regarding the on-exchange activities of large traders, including hedge funds, through its large trader reporting system and speculative position rules. However, even where the operator or advisor of a hedge fund may be registered as a CPO or CTA, the CFTC does not have extensive information about the off-exchange activities of the hedge fund. Similarly, CFTC-registered FCMs are not a useful source of information about hedge funds' activities in these other markets because they do not act as counterparty to such transactions, although they may have affiliates that do so.

APPENDIX D

THE SUPERVISION OF BANK EXPOSURE TO HEDGE FUNDS

1. Commercial Bank Relationships with Hedge Funds

Commercial bank relationships with hedge funds can involve direct lending, counterparty trading, direct equity investment in funds, investment advisory, and fund sales through private banking operations. The risks resulting from these activities are no different from the risks from similar activities with other types of financial institutions. However, the unique characteristics of hedge funds, such as dynamic trading strategies and frequent use of leverage, may alter the relative importance of different measurement and control elements that banks use for their risk management processes. This section of the appendix summarizes the scope of major bank exposures to hedge funds, identifies how examiners assess banks' credit risk management, and reviews the basic elements of the risk management systems used to manage these exposures. It also discusses lessons learned from the LTCM event, as well as from subsequent targeted reviews of banks' relationships with hedge funds.

Bank exposures to hedge funds

U.S. commercial bank activity with hedge funds, including exposure to the LTCM Fund, is concentrated in those money center institutions with major strategic business lines devoted to investment banking services and trading and derivatives activities. However, even at these institutions and the handful of other U.S. commercial banks identified to have such relationships, exposures to hedge funds represent a small portion of the aggregate credit exposure from both traditional banking and derivatives business lines. As of September 30, 1998, aggregate bank direct lending exposure to hedge funds is estimated at less than $4.3 billion at the twelve banks identified to have hedge fund relationships. This compares to total assets of more than $2.6 trillion at these institutions. U.S. commercial banks had estimated direct investments in hedge funds of less than $1.7 billion, including the recent workout investments in the LTCM Fund. While some banks do engage in repurchase agreement transactions with hedge funds, which can further increase credit exposure, this activity is limited given the constraints that the leverage ratio places on this business at U.S. commercial banks.

Most bank exposures with hedge funds arise from counterparty trading and derivatives activities. The estimated notional value of derivative contracts with hedge funds at money center banks with significant trading activities represents less than four percent of the total $27 trillion in total notional value of derivatives contracts at these institutions. The estimated current credit exposure of derivative positions with hedge funds amounted to less than four percent of the current credit exposure of all derivative positions at these institutions. Collateral held against current hedge fund exposures resulted in negligible net current credit exposure.

2. Supervision of Bank Credit Exposures to Hedge Funds

The banking agencies generally take a business line-oriented, risk-focused approach in conducting their supervisory activities. This approach is designed to conform with the operational structure and risk profile of the institutions supervised. The agencies focus supervisory resources on assessing the safety and soundness of the bank's activities. Examiners assess the level and direction of risk, and the quality of risk management for different types of risks (*e.g.*, credit, market, liquidity, operational, legal, reputation) on an aggregate basis. They also review risk profiles for various product offerings, business lines or activities (*e.g.*, lending, trading, investing, and derivatives). Accordingly, bank exposures from hedge funds are primarily supervised within the context of the functional area or product line in which they arise, such as lending or derivatives activities. Unless targeted for special review, exposures arising from any one type of customer or counterparty, such as hedge funds, are generally not singled out from other types of customers.

Supervisors expect banks to analyze hedge fund exposures consistent with the principles of sound credit risk management. Supervisors communicate these credit risk management principles via formal handbook guidance and periodic advisory letters to bankers and examiners. Supervisors have not had specific examination procedures for hedge fund exposures since it is not practical to have separate procedures for individual industries. Nevertheless, the guidance on sound practices as they relate to lending, trading, investing and derivatives activities are just as applicable to banks' hedge fund relationships as they are to any customer relationship.[1] Accordingly, supervisors use existing loan portfolio management, commercial loan, and counterparty trading examination guidance and procedures to assess the quantity of credit risk and quality of credit risk management processes. Bank supervisors, in recognition of some of the unique risks associated with counterparty trading exposures generally, and hedge funds particularly, have recently issued supplemental guidance for examiners to use in reviews of bank trading and dealer operations.[2]

In assessing compliance with sound practices, supervisors rely on continuous supervision of large complex banking organizations — which are the most likely institutions to have meaningful exposures to hedge funds. In general, supervisors assign examiners full time at these institutions to maintain an ongoing program of risk assessment, monitoring, and communications with bank management and directors. Supervisors rotate personnel selected for these assignments periodically to ensure that the staff maintains an objective and diverse supervisory perspective. Examiners assess the quality of banks' credit portfolios, which includes exposures from off-balance-sheet derivatives activities. They also evaluate the adequacy of credit risk management practices, through on-site reviews and from continuous supervision of credit exposures. In

---

[1] Such general guidance that is applicable to all types of counterparties includes OCC Banking Circular 277 and Advisory Letter 97-3 (Credit Underwriting Standards and Portfolio Credit Risk Measurement); and the Federal Reserve Board's Trading and Capital Markets Activities Manual and various supporting SR letters, including SR 93-69 and 97-17.

[2] See OCC Bulletin 99-2: Risk Management of Financial Derivatives and Bank Trading Activities, dated January 25, 1999; Federal Reserve SR letter 99-3: Supervisory Guidance Regarding Counterparty Credit Risk Management, dated February 1, 1999; Basle Committee on Banking Supervision: Banks' Interactions with Highly Leveraged Institutions (January 1999) and Sound Practices for Banks' Interactions with Highly Leveraged Institutions (January 1999).

choosing risk areas for targeted reviews, examiners emphasize those bank activities exhibiting higher than average risk or growth, and unique or new characteristics.

Hedge funds historically have not represented significant credit risk to banks, largely due to the collateralized nature of most transactions. The following discussion outlines how bank supervisors assess credit risk generally. It also discusses hedge fund exposures particularly, from the two principal sources of exposure: direct lending and counterparty trading. While the credit risk management of these two types of exposure to a hedge fund differ in important respects, they have many elements in common. Banks generally manage all types of exposures to a customer as a single credit relationship. Thus, the due diligence and monitoring described under direct lending applies also to counterparty trading, and banks are expected by supervisors to have comprehensive credit reporting systems that provide measures of total exposure to each hedge fund.

Supervision of direct lending activities

Examiners assess how bank management identifies, measures and controls risk throughout the credit process, by reviewing the bank's strategic direction, risk appetite, and risk management processes. Bank supervisors have not targeted hedge funds, as a separate industry class, for specific reviews. However, examiners have reviewed large hedge fund relationships as part of regular assessments of large exposures. For example, examiners evaluate hedge fund relationships as part of their targeted reviews of large corporate credits, including those exposures that fall under the scope of the Shared National Credit Program.[3]

When evaluating a targeted loan portfolio (*e.g.*, large corporate) and credit risk management practices, examiners consider the following specific factors, as appropriate, depending on the scope of the review:

Credit culture. Examiners evaluate the bank's credit culture because it exerts a strong influence on credit risk management. Values and behaviors that banks reward influence credit standards and can often take precedence over written policies and procedures. When practices do not correspond with policies, lenders may not clearly understand the culture, credit controls may not be effective, policies and systems may be inappropriate for the credit environment, or banks may reward employees for behaviors inconsistent with policy.

Loan policy. The loan policy is the primary means by which senior management and the board guide lending activities. Examiners assess whether the policy provides a framework for

---

[3] A shared national credit ("SNC") is any loan and/or formal commitment extended to a borrower by a supervised institution, or any of its subsidiaries or affiliates, which totals $20 million or more and: (1) is shared by three or more institutions under a formal lending agreement; or (2) a portion of which is sold to two or more institutions, where the purchasing institutions assume a pro-rata share of the credit risk.

achieving asset quality and earnings objectives, sets prudent risk tolerance levels and guides the bank's lending activities in a manner consistent with the bank's strategic direction.

Integrity and quality of the risk ratings process. Rating the credit risk of individual loans through regular credit evaluations is fundamental to a sound credit process. Such evaluations allow timely detection of changes in portfolio quality, and enable management to modify portfolio strategies and to intensify the supervision of weaker credits. Examiners review the bank's risk rating definitions and processes for reasonableness. To confirm the integrity of the risk rating process, examiners analyze individual credits to assess the quality of the risk rating analysis and to determine if management correctly assigns ratings. Examiners also assess whether the risk-rating framework provides sufficient guidelines for evaluating loans to entities with unique characteristics, such as leverage.

Loan approval process. The loan approval process is the first step towards ensuring sound portfolio credit quality. While examiners do not promote any particular system for loan approval, they evaluate whether the loan approval process introduces sufficient controls to ensure acceptable credit quality at origination. This process should be compatible with the bank's credit culture, risk profile, and capabilities of its credit personnel. Examiners evaluate whether the system for loan approvals establishes accountability for credit decisions.

Allowable types of loans. Examiners evaluate the types of loan relationships, including hedge funds, that the bank approves and evaluate them relative to the bank's ability to properly underwrite and supervise the credits. Because entities such as hedge funds may engage in sophisticated trading strategies, leveraging, and various off-balance-sheet activities, examiners assess whether the bank has retained personnel with the required expertise to analyze and monitor these specialized credits. The lending policy should control specific types of loans that have resulted in abnormal losses for the bank or that the bank considers to have less favorable risk/reward characteristics.

Underwriting criteria & due diligence reviews. Examiners assess a bank's underwriting standards on an ongoing basis through the review of individual credit files and changes to policy. Examiners assess the extent to which the credit analysis of individual exposures supports the underlying credit decision. These file reviews also help examiners assess compliance with policy and identify any deterioration in underwriting standards.

Examiners evaluate whether banks obtain sufficiently comprehensive financial and other information to provide a clear understanding of the obligor's risk profile. A sound underwriting process should contain the following elements, calibrated to the size of the obligor and the nature of their activities:

- Financial information, covering both on- and off-balance-sheet positions, including:
  - Current and historical balance-sheet and income data,
  - Balance-sheet, income, and cash flow projections, and
  - Comparative industry data.

- Sufficient detail about the major types of business strategies and activities to understand the obligor's overall risk profile, including the nature and size of the obligor's involvement in broad instrument categories and markets (cash, derivatives, leverage). For hedge funds, this should include a comprehensive, quantitative assessment of leverage and risk concentrations. To assess a hedge fund's leverage, for example, banks can compare the obligor's value-at-risk ("VaR") numbers and stress testing results to the amount of available capital. Even more straightforward statistics such as quarterly data on the standard deviation of daily P&L, or quarterly data on maximum daily loss or profit, have value for assessing risk.

- Sufficient understanding of the relative size of the obligor's aggregate positions in a given market, and the liquidity associated with these positions.

- Sufficient knowledge about, and risk assessments of, the obligor's performance on obligations with other creditors. A dealer's own transactions with a hedge fund might not reveal the fund's overall risk profile.

Because hedge funds actively trade and dynamically manage their investment positions, many of which can be off-balance-sheet, financial statements tend to have limited value in prospective credit analysis. Hedge funds view banks as competitors as well as creditors. Therefore, most hedge funds are very reluctant to share information on their trading strategies, a practical limitation which impairs the ability of the credit officer to gain comprehensive insight into the fund's risk profile. For these reasons, bank due diligence reviews of hedge fund customers tend to focus on more qualitative assessments of hedge fund credit quality, such as:

- the equity investment, track record and reputation of the principals;
- trading strategies and risk appetite;
- redemption policies;
- leverage, including for off-balance-sheet positions;
- the quality of risk management systems;
- front and back office operations; and
- offering circulars, private placement memorandums and partnership agreements.

Examiners then evaluate the effectiveness of banks' due diligence efforts and qualitative assessments. In particular, examiners review whether banks have established mitigating controls when the transparency of the hedge fund is inadequate. For example, hedge fund financial statements typically provide insufficient information to assess the risks of off-balance-sheet contracts, the effective degree of leverage, and changes in business strategies. Mitigating controls can include requiring collateral or negotiating more conservative covenants (especially contractual provisions that become more stringent as credit quality deteriorates) into credit agreements.

Because of increasing competitive pressures, banks had come under pressure to waive covenants. Examiners will investigate a high level of covenant waivers and assess the impact on loan quality and credit management practices. Examiners will also assess whether the underwriting policy sufficiently details procedures for approving exceptions to credit policies. Examiners evaluate the frequency of policy exceptions, an excessive level of which may indicate an unwarranted slippage in underwriting standards.

Examiners also determine that banks appropriately translate their risk tolerance levels into effective policies and procedures that deal both with individual as well as important classes of obligors. Policies, which reflect credit culture and risk appetite, need to drive the credit standard setting process, not competitive pressures in the marketplace. When bank management identifies credit concerns with regard to an obligor, it should take appropriate steps to limit and manage the exposure. For example, banks should either refuse to extend credit, or implement tougher credit conditions (*e.g.*, insist on more conservative financial covenants), for those obligors who provide less than complete information about their risk profile.

Ongoing monitoring. Banks typically impose on-going financial reporting requirements on hedge fund customers as part of their credit risk assessment and risk management process. Such reporting usually includes audited annual financial statements, quarterly financial statements, and monthly net asset value statements.

The variability of a hedge fund's financial position and risk profile, however, makes traditional tools of financial statement analysis less effective in assessing the credit exposure to a hedge fund. As noted in a 1994 BIS report on public disclosure of risks arising from trading activity, traditional accounting based information is not well suited to describing the risks associated with trading activity.[4] That report emphasized the importance of information about the volatility of trading portfolio values, both retrospectively and potentially, for assessing a counterparty's creditworthiness. While such information is produced by most risk management information systems, the degree to which that information is drawn upon in reports to trading

---

[4] Public Disclosure of Market and Credit Risks by Financial Intermediaries. Bank for International Settlements. September, 1994. The report recommended that "all financial intermediaries—regulated and unregulated—should move in the direction of disclosing periodic quantitative information which expresses, in summary form, the estimates relied upon by the firm's management of:

- the market risks in the relevant portfolio or portfolios, as well as the firm's actual performance in managing the market risks in these portfolios;
- the counterparty credit risks arising from its trading and risk management activities, including current and potential future credit exposure as well as counterparty creditworthiness, in a form which permits evaluation of the firm's performance in managing credit risk."

counterparties and other disclosures still varies widely. In general, hedge funds provide balance-sheet and income statements which are not informative about risk profiles.

Typically, banks receive only general information on the characteristics of a hedge fund's trading strategies (*e.g.*, aggressive growth, distressed securities, emerging markets, market neutral, etc.). Banks generally have not received the sort of risk-focused financial information, such as risk management reports or other summary measures of market and other risks (*e.g.*, liquidity and credit) that would allow for a more comprehensive credit assessment, particularly with respect to leverage. However, banks do look for changes in trading strategies. Banks can sometimes detect changes in strategy by observing trades placed with the banks' dealer operations. Deviations in a hedge fund's trading strategy can result in a fund straying from its area of market expertise, which can increase the bank's credit risk.

Given the limitations of the typical financial statement for timely assessment of a hedge fund's trading risks, banks and securities firms supplement traditional financial analysis with occasional on-site visits and qualitative evaluations of the fund's risk management practices, trading strategies, and performance. Such qualitative evaluations, while important, are not a substitute for better quantitative information.

Examiners evaluate the bank's process for monitoring client credit quality. Because of the dynamic nature of hedge fund trading activities, banks should require more frequent financial information on broad trading strategies, fund redemptions, leverage, and net asset values. Examiners evaluate whether banks obtain sufficient information, and review it with appropriate frequency, to demonstrate effective credit risk management.

Credit risk control function. Besides the loan policy, the primary controls over a bank's lending activities include credit administration, loan review, and audit functions. These units ensure the reliability and effectiveness of the bank's risk management process, management information systems ("MIS"), and internal and accounting controls. Control functions can also provide senior management and the board with a periodic assessment of how well the bank's employees understand the credit culture and whether their actions conform to the bank's standards and values.

During targeted credit examinations, examiners determine the scope and adequacy of banks' control functions, such as the loan review and audit functions. For example, examiners sample internal loan review workpapers and reports to assess their depth and coverage. To evaluate the competence of oversight functions, examiners will determine whether loan review personnel possess the required industry expertise to analyze loans to entities with unique characteristics, such as high leverage. Examiners also sample audit workpapers and reports to ensure that senior management is appropriately responsive to deficiencies and concerns cited by oversight units. Repeated deficiencies resulting from the failure to take appropriate corrective action prompt examiners to initiate discussions with, and seek corrective commitments from, executive management.

Supervision of counterparty trading exposure

For reasons mentioned earlier, supervisors generally have not targeted hedge funds, as a separate industry class, during reviews of counterparty risk from trading activities. Rather, supervisory efforts have focused on the largest counterparty credit exposures, and those exposures that are exceptions to bank policy.

The procedures for evaluating a bank's counterparty trading exposure and risk management systems are similar to the process described for evaluating direct lending activities. However, there are some unique issues that examiners consider when evaluating the credit risk management of counterparty exposures to leveraged entities, including hedge funds. Examiners consider:

Personnel. In order to effectively evaluate risk exposure and set appropriate credit limits, the personnel responsible for approving and monitoring counterparty credit exposure must possess a strong understanding of derivative instruments, the sources of credit exposure, and market factors that affect credit exposure. Credit personnel should receive ongoing training on derivative instruments, risk management techniques, and methods of measuring credit risk.

Counterparty limits. Banks should establish counterparty credit limits in much the same way as traditional credit lines. Counterparty credit limits should be a function of the bank's risk tolerance, the terms and conditions of financial contracts and, most importantly, the capacity of the counterparty to perform on its obligations. Limit approvals should precede the execution of derivative transactions. Credit file documentation should support the purpose, repayment source, and collateral.

For trading transactions, current credit exposure occurs when changes in market prices cause the replacement value (*i.e.*, current mark-to-market) of a transaction to rise above its value at inception.[5] A hedge fund default would cause a loss to a creditor if the current mark-to-market favored the creditor, because that creditor can replace the transaction only at the market prices prevailing after default.[6]

Counterparty credit risk includes both pre-settlement risk ("PSR") and settlement risk. Pre-settlement risk represents the current mark-to-market amount of counterparty positions, plus an estimate of potential future exposure ("PFE"), *i.e.*, how large that current mark-to-market might become over the life of the contract. The PFE reflects the possibility that the current credit exposure may increase as a result of *future* market movements. The PFE provides a measure of

---

[5] Almost all derivatives contracts have no current credit exposure at inception; the contract is priced fairly for each party.

[6] It is of course true that if the current mark-to-market is in favor of the hedge fund, then the hedge fund would suffer a loss if its creditor institution defaulted.

possible future changes in market value, at a specified confidence interval, over some defined horizon (typically over the life of the contract). PSR limits should be commensurate with the board's risk tolerance and the sophistication of the bank's risk measurement system. Banks which have less sophisticated credit risk measures should compensate by imposing more conservative limits.

Banks should have separate and distinct limits for settlement risk, which measures the exposures that occur when one party makes a payment prior to assurance that it has received a payment from its counterparty. Settlement risk lasts from the time a bank can no longer unilaterally cancel an outgoing payment until the time the bank receives the incoming payment with finality. Settlement risk arises because it is generally impractical to arrange simultaneous payment and delivery in the ordinary course of business. For example, settlement risk arises in international transactions because of time zone differences. This risk generally exists for a *minimum* of one to two days. It can take another one to two business days to confirm receipt through reconciliation procedures. As a result, settlement risk can accumulate during the reconciliation period, and span three business days (or more), until a bank can be certain that it has received a payment. A failure to perform may result from counterparty default, operational breakdown, or legal impediments. Settlement risk arises in both cash and off-balance-sheet derivatives dealing activities.

The dollar volume of exposure due to settlement risk sometimes is greater than the credit exposure arising from pre-settlement risk because settlement can involve an exchange of the total notional value of the instrument or principal cash flow. Limits should reflect the credit quality of the counterparty and the bank's own capital adequacy, operations efficiency, and credit expertise. Any transaction that will exceed a limit should be pre-approved by an appropriate credit officer. Reports to managers should enable them to easily recognize limit excesses.

Stress testing. Banks need to stress test their credit, as well as market, risk profiles in order to evaluate the potential impact of adverse market conditions on cash flows and asset/collateral values supporting trading transactions. Stress testing helps identify those counterparties likely to create the greatest credit exposures in market environments more severe than standard risk measurement methods assume. Examiners place increasing emphasis with banks on the need to stress test counterparty trading exposures as a supplement to routine (normal case) estimation of pre-settlement risk. If stress testing identifies particularly risky positions, the bank should consider reducing exposure, or requiring additional collateral.

Examiners also assess whether the bank has considered the impact of liquidating collateral in the event the borrower defaults. The potential for disorderly liquidation, financial market disruption, and systemic market stress is a function of the borrower's leverage, the concentration of collateral in any one market, and prevailing market conditions. Disorderly markets increase credit risk because banks may not realize sufficient value upon collateral liquidation to completely offset their current credit exposures. Because hedge funds are active participants in many financial markets, and frequently rely on leverage, banks face greater risks of having to liquidate collateral in disorderly conditions with hedge funds than with many other trading counterparties.

Collateral management. Given the information problems associated with hedge funds, leverage, and the volatility of hedge fund net asset values, banks and securities firms usually require collateral on their trading exposures to hedge funds. Generally, banks require collateral to cover the current credit exposure or current replacement value. Banks normally require a "haircut" (collateral margin) when financing a counterparty's acquisition of a trading asset, such as in reverse repurchase agreements. Competitive pressures, however generally led to banks' reducing, or eliminating such haircuts, and thus sometimes banks have provided 100% financing. For over-the-counter derivatives, many hedge fund clients negotiated loss thresholds in their trading agreements.[7] Loss thresholds are small, generally less than $5 million. To reduce the need for frequent small transfers of collateral, the trading agreements often set minimum collateral transfers to trigger collateral calls above the thresholds. These minimum transfer amounts are even smaller. The unsecured exposure thus can total the amount of the threshold plus the minimum transfer requirement. While loss thresholds and minimum transfer amounts are also subject to strong competitive pressure, on balance, banks generally have had well collateralized current credit exposures to hedge funds.

Examiners evaluate the potential risks in smaller collateral haircuts, and the size of loss thresholds, in relation to the overall credit quality of the relationship and the grace period for posting collateral. Collateral agreements typically include a close-out provision allowing the bank to terminate a client's positions if it is unable to post the required collateral within a specified grace period. These close-out provisions may or may not allow recourse back to the counterparty. A non-recourse close-out could lead to losses for the bank if the underlying positions are illiquid.

Due to the increasing trend of collateralizing derivative transactions, examiners assess the operational integrity of collateral monitoring systems as part of their review of back office operations. During these reviews, examiners look at collateral perfection, initial account set up, how collateral is held in accordance with documentation (including controls on collateral segregation and rehypothecation/substitution of collateral), and adequacy of collateral haircuts. Examiners assess how the bank ensures accurate mark-to-market valuation of trading counterparty positions in order to determine collateral coverage and make collateral calls if necessary. They also review the level of disputes with counterparties as an indicator of whether there is a recurring problem with the price marks. Some warning of problems may occur through the spotting of irregularities in a customer's posting of collateral.

---

[7] A loss threshold represents current mark-to-market exposure below which a bank agrees not to require collateral. It represents unsecured credit exposure. For example, a bank might grant a hedge fund a $1 million loss threshold. This means that the fund would post collateral only after the current replacement cost of the contract exceeds $1 million.

Examiners assess whether banks regularly compare trading exposures against collateral pledged by the counterparty. Depending upon the volatility of the underlying positions and liquidity of the collateral, banks may need to do this on an intra day basis. Examiners also evaluate the timeliness of collateral calls when the current credit exposure exceeds the value of collateral. Examiners review the grace period allowed to post margin and the history of fails to assess the bank's potential risk exposure. They may test individual transactions to determine if the bank made collateral calls in accordance with policy.

Examiners affirm that banks have in place clearly articulated policies for the establishment of collateral arrangements with counterparties. Policies should lay out clear guidelines for the type of collateral arrangements required, based on criteria such as the rating assigned to the counterparty, the quality of information available, and the nature, volatility and liquidity of the transactions. In particular, banks need to have clear internal guidelines detailing the types of acceptable collateral and their respective haircuts, as well as the condition under which the bank will require collateral to cover some portion of the PFE of trading transactions. Finally, the granting of two-way collateral arrangements, and any re-hypothecation rights given to the counterparty, should be a function of the obligor's credit quality and the bank's own liquidity position. Examiners evaluate whether audit and other oversight units regularly evaluate the adequacy of the collateral management function as well as test compliance with established policies and procedures.

Documentation exceptions. Trading documentation refers broadly to the documents needed to legally enforce the credit agreement and properly analyze the borrower's financial capacity. When a document is missing, stale, or improperly executed, it becomes an exception. Documentation exceptions can exacerbate problem exposures and seriously hamper work-out efforts. For example, failure to ensure timely receipt and analysis of financial information can preclude the early identification of potential problems and the opportunity to initiate efforts to strengthen the credit. Failure to promptly review financial information can delay exercising any powers to strengthen the creditor's position under the credit agreement. Examiners will analyze the level, composition, and trend of documentation exceptions to assess potential risks.

Maintaining current documentation of all outstanding contracts is an important component of credit risk management. Generally, signed master agreements are required prior to initiation of trading transactions. Where master agreements have not been signed, "full" confirmations containing many of the provisions found in a master agreement are used. Master agreements usually include standard ISDA (International Swaps and Derivatives Association) and IFEMA (International Foreign Exchange Master Agreement) default clauses, supplemented with additional termination events covering the dissolution or liquidation of the fund, the resignation of the fund's general partner or principals, or decreases in net asset values beyond a certain threshold.

Interconnection risk. Recent market events have underscored the importance of assessing risk interconnections. For example, market and credit risks are directly related. When a contract moves deeply into-the-money for the bank, counterparty credit risk increases. Similarly, as credit risk increases across the system, liquidity tends to erode, making it more difficult for the bank to manage the risk of its portfolios. Counterparties having deeply out-of-the money positions may threaten litigation, asserting that the bank has not sufficiently disclosed all contract risks, especially if the contract involves a high degree of complexity. Examiners also focus on the bank's client selection process to determine if management has properly considered reputation and potential litigation risks. Bank management, with the strong encouragement of supervisors, have been working to identify and develop analytical responses to interconnection risk.

Use of risk measurement models. In addition to the core examination staff, supervisors increasingly use economists, who hold PhDs in economics or finance, to assist in trading examinations. Economists help to assess theoretical and quantitative issues in the models banks use for pricing and risk management.

Examiners assess whether bank management places undue reliance on quantitative risk modeling techniques. Although financial modeling has proven to be a valuable risk management tool, such models have limitations. Banks must complement risk models with sound risk management practices, especially a stress testing program, and appropriate risk oversight by experienced personnel.

Control of legal risk. Because the enforceability of many OTC derivative contracts has not been tested in the courts in all jurisdictions, examiners evaluate whether banks employ competent legal counsel to review applicable documents prior to executing transactions, and periodically thereafter. Counsel should be familiar with the economic substance of the transaction, the laws of the jurisdictions in which the parties reside, and laws governing the market in which the instrument was traded. When a bank does not use standardized documents, or makes changes to standardized contracts, examiners assess whether bank counsel has reviewed the documents and/or changes for propriety. When the legal enforceability of netting arrangements is not certain, examiners also ensure that bank management measures credit exposures on a gross basis, to avoid understating credit risk.

3. Credit Risk Management Issues

Lessons learned from LTCM

Although the liquidation of direct exposures to the LTCM Fund could have significantly impacted quarterly earnings at several banking institutions, it would not have threatened the solvency of any U.S. commercial bank. Nevertheless, the favorable credit terms given to the LTCM Fund by some banks despite a lack of information about the full scope of the LTCM Fund's exposures raises important questions regarding the credit risk management processes at these institutions. Such questions pertain to the management of not only hedge fund relationships, but also other types of trading counterparties.

The root of any breakdowns in the credit risk management systems of banking institutions in the LTCM incident result from imbalances in the dynamic interactions of the basic credit risk management elements described above, in particular, an over reliance on collateral to mitigate and control credit risk. In managing the LTCM relationship and relationships with some other hedge funds, banks clearly relied on significantly less information on the financial strength, condition, and liquidity of their counterparty than is available for, and perhaps required of, other types of counterparties. Banks relied on the protection provided by the collateralization of the current replacement cost of trading exposures to offset the compromises made in their credit risk management programs. While collateral can help to reduce credit risk, it does so at the expense of increased liquidity, operational and legal risks. Moreover, in disorderly markets, a deterioration in collateral values can result in the collateral value failing to cover current credit exposures, creating credit losses.

Specific weaknesses in counterparty credit risk management and supervisory responses

Credit exposure measurement standards. In measuring and managing derivative exposures with the LTCM Fund and other hedge funds, banks relied primarily on the timely collateralization of the current market value of their exposures. Although the LTCM incident did not expose major difficulties in the operation of collateral management systems, the specific measures used to assess potential credit exposure to the LTCM Fund, and more generally for other collateralized counterparties, require enhancements.

Banks generally calculate derivatives and foreign exchange exposure as the sum of current market exposure and potential future exposure ("PFE"). Most banks calculate PFEs using a holding period reflecting the remaining life of the contract and often estimate the peak exposure over the contract's life. At some banking institutions these methodologies have generated such conservative measures that they failed to be a meaningful representation of exposure. In addition, meaningful comparisons between exposures in the loan portfolio and those in the derivatives book become difficult. As a result, credit officers and traders are less likely to use PFEs as a tool to manage credit exposures, and therefore tend to rely heavily on the current market exposure. For example, when banks established credit limits based upon the results of a highly conservative PFE calculation, such "limits" not only overstate risk but they also do not represent the degree of current market exposure a bank would willingly accept. Instead, limits are set at the levels necessary to accommodate the hedge fund's current business volumes, rather than as a constraint imposed as a result of sound credit analysis and judgment.

In addition, life-of-contract measures of PFE vastly overstate the exposure to collateralized counterparties. The use of lifetime PFEs *overstates* the potential exposure when banks mark-to-market their positions daily and have the ability to close-out the counterparty's position, *e.g.*, if the counterparty fails to post sufficient collateral. Notwithstanding the collateralized nature of the credit agreement, a bank still has measurable unsecured credit exposure to its collateralized counterparties arising from the lag between the issuance of a margin call and the posting of margin. A bank's actual credit exposure in a collateralized relationship, in which the bank can call for additional collateral as the current mark-to-market increases, is the PFE from the time a counterparty fails to meet a collateral call until the time the bank liquidates its collateral and/or hedges its exposure. This period is typically much shorter than the contract's life.

Recent events have illustrated that banks need to define more effective PFEs, particularly for collateralized counterparty relationships. The PFE measure for collateralized counterparties should consider the liquidity of derivatives instruments, the near-term volatility of their potential values, and more realistic time frames in which banks can take risk reducing actions.

In addition, the approach to aggregating PFEs for a given counterparty can influence the conservatism of the exposure measures. Banks can aggregate PFEs for a given counterparty using a transaction approach or a portfolio approach. Under the transaction approach, banks calculate exposure to the counterparty as the simple sum of the potential exposures for each transaction. Since the transaction approach assumes that all transactions will achieve their estimated exposure at the same time, it typically overstates aggregate "portfolio" risk to the counterparty. For example, consider a hedge fund with both long and short interest rate swap positions with a bank. The transaction approach might sum the peak exposures, whenever they occur. As a result, it would add credit exposures for contracts even though they represent offsetting market positions.

Some banks use a "portfolio" approach to measure potential credit exposure. The portfolio approach addresses the overstatement of credit risk generated by the transaction approach by using simulation modeling to calculate exposures across products and transactions through time for the counterparty. The model incorporates both correlations among transaction factors and contractual close-out netting. It therefore provides a lower, yet more accurate, measure of credit risk.

Some institutions already calculate PFEs by assessing the estimated worst case value of positions over a time horizon of one or two weeks and incorporate cross product netting and correlation portfolio effects to construct a comprehensive measure of exposure to a collateralized counterparty. This allows such banks to more realistically define their credit risk exposures, assuming the bank faces no impediments (legal or otherwise) to liquidating collateral.

Moving forward, supervisors should encourage institutions to implement more realistic PFE calculations, using more appropriate measures of exposure within a generally more consistent exposure measurement framework (including loan exposures) and based upon a portfolio (as opposed to a transaction) approach. A single measure of PFE may not be sufficient for managing credit risk, and several measures, including PFEs calculated for different holding periods, may be helpful. Supervisors' experience suggests that conservatism in statistical measures of exposure is better achieved by greater precision than by overestimation. Such enhanced calculations would clearly facilitate and enable more disciplined limit structures and counterparty exposure management processes, and provide greater integrity to the entire credit process.

Stress testing. Currently, banks' procedures for stress testing their counterparty credit exposures are not as well developed as for market risk exposures. Many banks do not have adequate credit stress testing procedures, typically due to systems problems. Fragmented systems at large internationally active banks make it difficult to aggregate information. Recent events demonstrate that credit exposures change rapidly as market volatility increases. Although a bank may believe that it has a reasonably well-secured exposure, extreme price movements and disorderly markets can quickly lead to an unanticipated exposure. Banks need to stress test their counterparty credit portfolios to identify individual counterparties, or groups of counterparties, with positions that are particularly vulnerable to extreme or one-way directional market movements. Through stress testing, better-managed banks may identify risk issues, such as concentrations in collateral, that jeopardize the bank's collateral protection across its hedge fund client base and therefore warrant further investigation.

It is important to note that even the ostensibly conservative life-of-contract measures of PFE are not genuine stress tests, in that they are not based on assumptions of volatile markets, reductions of transaction volumes and higher than normal liquidation costs arising from disorderly markets. They do not factor in the follow-on effects of a default by a major collateralized counterparty, such as a hedge fund, which would force a bank to liquidate positions and re-balance its market risk portfolio. Potential losses in such events are a function of market liquidity, which can erode rapidly if multiple counterparties experience problems or choose to de-leverage rapidly. Supervisors should encourage institutions to consider such factors in their stress testing exercises. Finally, historical data may insufficiently gauge the potential for true stress events in any given market. Thus, risk managers should identify and develop appropriately severe "what if" scenarios throughout their portfolio. At present, it appears that few institutions conduct such scenario stress testing.

Banks have looked primarily to their daily collateral management systems as a means to manage and control their credit exposures. Updated supervisory guidance in this area may be especially pertinent.

Due diligence process. Banks' due diligence for hedge funds may have been less than adequate due both to a reluctance of funds to share basic information with the banks and an individual bank's interest in conducting business with the fund. The rigor of the due diligence process has much to do with the institution's corporate credit culture, as described earlier.

In the interest of conducting transactions, banks may set counterparty credit limits based on customer demand and line usage, as opposed to rigorous assessments of default probabilities and exposures. Banks clearly have relied on significantly less information on the financial strength, condition, and liquidity of their hedge fund counterparties than is available for, and perhaps required of, other types of counterparties. Insufficient information to conduct meaningful due diligence and assess counterparty default probabilities should result in lower counterparty credit limits, or downward adjustment of existing limits, and requirements for greater collateral. If the information deficit is great enough, banks should decline to enter trading relationships with the counterparty, and some have indeed done so. Banks should have policies in place governing the terms of credit, such as unsecured threshold amounts, haircuts on repurchase agreements, two-way collateral agreements and collateral requirements to cover some or all of the short horizon estimate of PFE, to be offered counterparties based on the information provided and the underlying credit quality and liquidity of the counterparty. While banks tightened credit terms on derivatives and negotiated stronger financial disclosure covenants in their loan agreements as a result of troubled markets last fall, the soundness of credit terms offered to hedge funds remains an area of supervisory concern.

In general, banks seem to have displayed the following shortcomings with regard to conducting appropriate due diligence of hedge funds:

- When assessing the financial condition of the hedge funds, banks did not fully analyze off-balance-sheet information. When banks did, they often assessed derivatives on a net, not gross, basis, and therefore underestimated the sheer size of LTCM's transactions volume. In addition, banks did not have a complete understanding of the risk profile of hedge funds because they seldom could get information incorporating transactions done with other dealers.

- Rapid market changes required hedge funds to change their risk profile significantly, leaving typical financial analysis outdated in a short time period. Banks needed to obtain more risk-focused financial information, such as risk management reports detailing a fund's value at risk and an assessment of exposures in stressed market environments.

- Banks did not understand or assess the adequacy of the liquidity risk management approaches of hedge funds, especially those funds, such as LTCM, which relied heavily on collateral to obtain financing.

- During the LTCM experience, banks found they wanted to make more frequent collateral calls with a shorter time to post collateral, given a rapidly changing environment. However, trading agreements sometimes stood in the way. For example, the standard ISDA master agreement has a two-day lag following mark-to-market of the position.

- Banks frequently use the personal investment of principals in hedge funds as a gauge of financial support, but this indicator proved to be less useful than expected since some fund managers used borrowed funds to make the investment.

- Banks may have relied on the track record of hedge fund managers too heavily, focusing on past performance rather than consideration of future potential and risk. The highly leveraged nature of hedge funds, and their dynamic trading strategies, made frequent assessments of counterparty credit quality more important than for other borrower classes.

- Banks may have placed too much reliance on the strategies articulated by hedge fund managers, and/or assumed that "market neutral" strategies entailed less risk. The nature of bank monitoring did not allow the banks to detect significant changes in strategy early enough. Banks' assessment of the quality of risk management systems may have relied too heavily on the people associated with risk management and not enough on actual understanding of the tools used to control risk. Some hedge fund trading strategies frequently rely heavily on the use of models, and all hedge funds should be able to provide summary measures of market, credit and liquidity risk, which banks need to understand and analyze.

Supervisors should closely monitor banks' efforts to address the weaknesses in due diligence processes discussed above and in recent supervisory guidance, including bank managements' use of on-site visits to assess funds' risk management capabilities.

The due diligence process for analyzing proposed business with hedge funds should not differ fundamentally from other sound business selection procedures. Two areas in particular require additional care. Specifically:

- Banks should not compromise their business selection process as a result of the unwillingness of potential hedge fund counterparties to provide all necessary information. In the credit process for loans, for example, the borrower's unwillingness to provide essential information is generally sufficient to turn down a loan application.

- Banks should make use as needed of covenants or similar provisions to ensure that they can closely monitor credit exposures to hedge funds. Documentation supporting on-balance-sheet exposures to hedge funds already typically contains covenants that require the hedge fund to notify lenders of material changes in its financial condition and, in extreme circumstances, allow the bank to declare an event of default and seek early repayment. Scope almost certainly exists to incorporate covenant-like provisions in the documentation supporting OTC derivatives that would entitle banks to obtain and monitor key features of hedge funds' financial strength, including factors pertaining to leverage. Such provisions would, however, require careful design in order to ensure that the information provided about the hedge fund and the conditionality over the facility is meaningful.

Closeout provisions. In general, most banks use standard ISDA (International Swaps and Derivatives Association) documentation and have closeout rights that allow the banks to closeout contracts if the financial condition of a counterparty becomes significantly impaired. For hedge funds, a standard closeout provision is one based on declines in net asset value ("NAV"). While the standard NAV closeout trigger for most hedge funds is a 20 percent drop in NAV, several large hedge funds, including the LTCM Fund, brought competitive pressures to bear in order to gain 40-50 percent NAV declines as their closeout provision. This obviously reduces the capital cushion available at closeout events.

On the surface, the use of NAV closeout provisions seems eminently reasonable. However, on closer review, it appears that many of these closeout provisions are based on annual returns calculated either at year-end or on a 12 month rolling average basis. Given the potential smoothing of near-term poor performance by performance in prior months, triggers having this structure may be late or misleading signals of problems and the actions triggered may be untimely and ineffective mitigators of risk. For a fund in deteriorating financial condition, a bank may not be able to execute closeout provisions for up to 12 months after the deterioration began. In this regard, institutions should ensure that when they negotiate closeout provisions, they employ prudent triggers that allow timely action in the event of a meaningful deterioration in the financial condition of a counterparty.

Beyond NAV thresholds, banks generally did not have flexible contractual provisions that could become more stringent as the credit quality of the counterparty deteriorates. For example, banks might require the posting of collateral, or increases in collateral haircuts, as the counterparty's risk profile changes.

Ongoing monitoring. Banks may also need to enhance ongoing exposure monitoring. With some large hedge fund counterparties, banks received only rudimentary monthly balance sheets and monthly changes in fund net asset values. The net asset values appear to be the primary monitoring tool used by most banks. Supervisors should encourage institutions to use more robust monitoring tools and require more complete, and current, information from their counterparties. When hedge funds will not provide such information, banks should compensate with more conservative credit structures and/or refuse to provide credit.

Given the LTCM Fund and its ability to amass potential market-moving shares of individual instruments and markets, banking institutions are paying more attention to potential market concentration measures in assessing their exposures to hedge funds. However, banks should consider expanding such measures to include other types of financial institutions. Supervisors should encourage the development of exposure measures that take into account possible market concentration and liquidity impacts to all counterparty credit exposures.

Credit exposure management process. Credit assessments of hedge funds are likely to have relatively short shelf lives — a fact that arises out of the nature of their businesses. Banks can reasonably expect credit assessments of most industrial companies to fairly represent a company's financial condition for up to one year because of the relative stability of most businesses. The same applies to mainstream financial institutions, which tend to be comparatively transparent, benefit from more diverse funding and revenue sources, and are subject to various forms of external supervision. Credit assessments of hedge funds, however, can become outdated very quickly given the dynamic nature of their business and, because of their leverage, their vulnerability to changing market conditions. A more volatile risk profile, combined with the absence of external monitoring (*e.g.*, by credit rating agencies), demands that banks update their internal assessments of hedge fund credit quality more frequently.

Bank supervisors may wish to review existing guidance with regard to the internal ratings of derivative counterparties, the setting of counterparty credit limits, and the overall exposure monitoring and limit exception process. The lack of granularity that supervisors have identified based on a study of internal loan ratings systems for commercial loans may easily carry-over into the rating of derivative counterparties.[8] In general, it appears that many institutions group counterparty ratings into only one or two rating categories, thus allowing for relatively little differentiation with respect to credit quality. The lack of risk rating granularity may make it more difficult for banks to incorporate more conservative covenants into credit agreements that reflect potentially meaningful distinctions in hedge fund credit quality.

Liquidity Risk of Counterparties. All banks place significant emphasis on collateral in managing their derivative exposures with hedge funds. The ability of hedge funds to meet margin calls as necessary is therefore an important consideration for banks in the credit process. For most large hedge funds, two-way collateral arrangements appear standard. Most of these two-way arrangements also provide for rehypothecation of collateral, *i.e.*, they allow the party holding the collateral to re-pledge it. Counterparties find these provisions useful in the day-to-day management of their liquidity risk.

The importance of collateral to hedge funds and other leveraged counterparties in maintaining market access represents a substantial liquidity risk which must be measured, monitored and carefully managed by the counterparty. Careful management includes development of an adequate liquidity contingency plan, all the more so when day-to-day liquidity is managed aggressively, with few liquidity buffers. In addition, the liquidity risk of a hedge fund interacts with and is magnified by leverage, most clearly in distressed market circumstances.

The need to identify and control the risk that a counterparty's liquidity vulnerabilities exacerbate its credit risk points to the importance of assessing liquidity risk management as part of the general due diligence and credit assessment of leveraged counterparties such as hedge funds. Bank managements generally need to strengthen attention to this aspect of their counterparties' risk profiles. In addition, the level of the counterparty's liquidity risk and the

---

[8] William F. Treacy and Mark S. Carey, "Credit Risk Rating at Large U.S. Banks." *Federal Reserve Bulletin* (November 1998).

effectiveness of liquidity risk management should be important factors in deciding on the appropriate credit terms for counterparties, including the terms of collateral arrangements.

Conclusion

The LTCM Fund was, to a large extent, an exception with regard to both the amount of leverage employed and the lack of information it provided to creditor banks. At the same time, LTCM seems the extreme case that illustrates the inherent weaknesses of some prevailing credit practices. Importantly, the lessons learned regarding the measurement, monitoring, and management of counterparty credit risks arising from this incident are generally applicable to the management of all derivatives transactions. Overall, the factors underlying the LTCM incident in particular, and the current state of banks' relationships with hedge funds in general, bear some resemblance to past commercial bank excesses such as the real estate phenomenon of the late 1980s and early 1990s. The confluence of competitive pressures, pursuit of earnings, and personal and professional relationships may have led some institutions to suspend or ignore fundamental risk management principles regarding counterparty due diligence, exposure monitoring, and the management of credit risk limits. Some large institutions need to enhance their counterparty credit risk exposure measurement and management regimes. Supervisors must remain alert to the conditions which can lead institutions to suspend prudent risk management practices, and tailor their supervisory efforts to require institutions to correct risk management weaknesses so as to reduce the likelihood that such weaknesses will pose a systemic threat.

APPENDIX E

BANKRUPTCY ISSUES

1. Background

The immediate termination and subsequent liquidation of the OTC derivatives, futures, and repurchase transactions of the foreign hedge fund Long-Term Capital Portfolio, L.P. (the "LTCM Fund" or "Fund"), which was managed by Long-Term Capital Management, L.P. "LTCM") through its Connecticut offices, would have probably generated significant movements in market prices and rates with resulting increased losses for the LTCM Fund's counterparties and, potentially, for other market participants as well. The adoption of the consortium approach by a number of the LTCM Fund's counterparties likely prevented this scenario from occurring.

U.S., U.K., and Cayman Islands law provide extensive statutory protection for close-out netting in insolvency. The U.S. Bankruptcy Code and other relevant insolvency statutes generally permit parties to certain defined financial contracts to enforce contractual provisions permitting the termination of those contracts and the netting of the amounts due upon the insolvency of their counterparty. As a result, the LTCM Fund's counterparties could reduce their individual credit and market risk by immediately closing out their positions with the Fund.[1]

In cases of insolvency, the availability of close-out netting enhances market stability by limiting losses to solvent counterparties, by reducing precipitous terminations of contracts, and by preserving liquidity for the solvent counterparties. This ability to terminate financial contracts upon a counterparty's insolvency thus preserves liquidity and permits the solvent party to replace the terminated contract without incurring additional market risk. Netting reduces the counterparty risk to financial institutions and thus reduces the "systemic" risks that the failure of one financial institution will cause a "domino" effect on other institutions and disrupt the financial markets. Bank supervisors have recognized the importance of close-out netting in reducing systemic risk to the financial system and have incorporated that recognition into advantageous capital treatment in U.S. and international bank capital regulations. The Basle Capital Accord similarly recognizes those benefits.

However, the LTCM Fund's significant positions in certain markets and the condition of those markets created the potential for a much greater impact on the markets in the event of immediate termination and subsequent liquidation of the LTCM Fund's financial contracts. As a consequence of the large, and in some cases extremely large, positions held by the LTCM Fund in certain markets, the simultaneous liquidation of those positions by its counterparties before and after a declaration of bankruptcy potentially could have created disruptions and heightened volatility in the financial markets. The reason is that all of the LTCM Fund's counterparties would have been trying to promptly liquidate their collateral while simultaneously attempting to close out their positions and reestablish their hedges relating to any defaulted contracts.

---

[1] As discussed in greater detail below, however, it is possible that the liquidation of U.S. collateral pledged by the LTCM Fund to its counterparties could have been affected by Section 304 of the U.S. Bankruptcy Code.

2. The U.S. Legal Framework's Treatment of Derivative Contracts in Insolvencies

Under U.S. law, different statutes govern the insolvencies of different types of financial market participants. The Bankruptcy Code governs insolvency proceedings for most corporations, partnerships and limited liability companies, while the Securities Investor Protection Act of 1971 (in conjunction with the Bankruptcy Code) governs insolvency proceedings involving stockbrokers who are members of the Securities Investor Protection Corporation. Insolvencies of insured banks and thrifts are governed by the bank receivership provisions of the Federal Deposit Insurance Act ("FDIA"), the National Bank Act, and, for state-chartered institutions, state law. The Federal Credit Union Act includes provisions, similar to those in the FDIA, covering the insolvency treatment of financial contracts by federally-insured credit unions. In 1991, Congress enacted the Federal Deposit Insurance Corporation Improvement Act of 1991 ("FDICIA"), which included provisions governing the treatment of netting contracts between financial institutions.

Congress has taken steps to enhance the availability of netting for derivatives and to minimize the risk of systemic events. For example, both the Bankruptcy Code and the FDIA contain provisions that protect the rights of financial participants to terminate certain types of financial contracts following the bankruptcy or insolvency of a counterparty to such contracts or agreements. Furthermore, other provisions prevent transfers made under such circumstances from being avoided as preferences or fraudulent conveyances (except when made with actual intent to defraud). Protections also are afforded under U.S. law to ensure that the netting, set off and collateral foreclosure provisions of such transactions and master agreements for such transactions are enforceable. Finally, FDICIA protects the enforceability of close-out netting provisions in "netting contracts" between "financial institutions."[2] FDICIA states that the goal of enforcing netting arrangements is to reduce systemic risk within the banking system and financial markets.

However, in the case of the LTCM Fund, U.S. bankruptcy law may not have governed its winding up since any bankruptcy proceeding would have, to a certain extent, occurred in the Cayman Islands.[3] Although LTCM was a Delaware limited partnership, the LTCM Fund itself was a Cayman limited partnership. It is very likely, therefore, that the LTCM Fund would have sought bankruptcy protection in the Cayman Islands. If so, it is quite possible that any U.S.

---

[2] These terms are broadly defined. A "financial institution" includes broker-dealers, depository institutions, future commissions merchants, and other entities recognized by Federal Reserve regulation. On March 7, 1994, the Federal Reserve expanded the definition of "financial institution" to include many significant participants in the financial markets. See Regulation EE, 12 CFR Part 231.

[3] As the sole general partner of the Fund, another Cayman Islands limited partnership, Long-Term Capital Portfolio (GP), L.P. ("GP1"), would have been legally obligated to the extent the LTCM Fund's liabilities exceeded its assets. A Cayman limited liability company, Long-Term Capital Portfolio (GP), Ltd. ("GP2"), would also have been indirectly liable for all of the LTCM Fund's obligations because it was liable for the obligations of GP1 as the sole general partner of GP1. As a result, any Cayman Islands insolvency proceeding would have been likely to also involve these two other entities. (We note that GP2 is controlled by Long-Term Capital Management, L.P.)

bankruptcy proceeding could have been merely ancillary in nature.[4] In addition, since the LTCM Fund entered into over-the-counter transactions in financial markets throughout the world, its financial assets were held in a variety of countries and any insolvency proceedings involving the Fund would have been affected by how the law of those countries treated contractual rights to closeout and net financial contracts and liquidate related collateral as well as the extent to which the laws of those countries would defer to foreign insolvency proceedings with respect to assets held in those countries. At a minimum, substantial legal uncertainty remained for counterparties and other creditors of the Fund because bankruptcy proceedings may very well have been initiated both in the U.S. and abroad and involved resolution of complicated and novel international bankruptcy issues.

In short, it is impossible to determine with complete precision how the LTCM Fund's various contracts would have been treated if an insolvency had occurred. Nevertheless, most financial market participants structure their relationships with their counterparties to provide for closeout, netting, and collateral liquidation through contractual provisions, including choice of law provisions. Moreover, in the event of an actual insolvency, because of the economic incentives, many counterparties may simply act and litigate the legitimacy of that action later. Accordingly, for the sake of simplicity, this discussion assumes that the U.S. Bankruptcy Code would be the applicable law while also briefly addressing the implications if the Fund's U.S. bankruptcy proceeding was ancillary in nature.

The treatment of financial contracts under the Bankruptcy Code

The Bankruptcy Code gives creditors a broad right to file a involuntary bankruptcy petition against debtors regardless of where the debtor is incorporated so long as such action is brought where the debtor's assets or principal place of business are located. As a result, with respect to foreign limited partnerships such as the LTCM Fund and its Cayman affiliates, an involuntary petition could have been initially filed under the Bankruptcy Code by creditors of the Fund and its affiliated entities.

When a bankruptcy petition is filed, an automatic stay is imposed which generally prohibits any action to collect debts owed by the bankrupt party, including netting or termination of outstanding contracts.[5] This stay does not eliminate the contractual right to net, but it does bar the immediate exercise of those rights. During this stay, netting can be exercised only if the contract qualifies under one of the five defined types of financial contracts protected under the

---

[4] While it is also quite possible that the Fund's U.S. creditors would have filed an involuntary bankruptcy petition against the Fund in the U.S. and a U.S. bankruptcy court would have been able to exert jurisdiction over the Fund, whether the U.S. court would have stayed its hand in deference to a Cayman Islands bankruptcy proceeding is unclear.

[5] Section 365(e)(1) prohibits the termination of most contracts by mere virtue of bankruptcy, financial condition or the like. Such termination provisions are commonly referred to as "ipso facto" clauses.

Bankruptcy Code or if the counterparty obtains bankruptcy court approval pursuant to Section 362(d). The Bankruptcy Code also grants to the trustee expansive powers to avoid pre-bankruptcy transfers — for example, payments or other property — and require the return of the transferred property to the bankruptcy estate. Although the Bankruptcy Code generally permits the set-off or netting of pre-petition mutual debts, it bars set-off during the 90 day period preceding bankruptcy if the creditor received more through the set-off than the pro rata share of the bankruptcy estate it would otherwise have received.[6] The bankruptcy trustee also has broad powers to avoid fraudulent transfers, which include those made for less than reasonably equivalent value while the bankrupt entity was insolvent or in otherwise severe financial difficulties as described in the Bankruptcy Code.[7] These provisions are designed to support the bankruptcy principle that all creditors are to be treated equally.

In order to reduce systemic risks, however, Congress has provided statutory exceptions from many of these restrictions for repurchase agreements, securities contracts, commodity contracts, swap agreements, and forward contracts. The Bankruptcy Code's provisions thus protect eligible entities from losses that could result from market fluctuations if the eligible entities were unable to terminate and net these derivatives during the bankruptcy proceeding. The bank insolvency laws, which are primarily found in the FDI Act, also provide similar "safe harbors" to protect the liquidity of these five types of financial contracts despite the insolvency of a bank or thrift counterparty.

Under the Bankruptcy Code, there are four principal benefits available to a party to one of the defined derivatives contracts. First, the party can terminate the contract despite the Bankruptcy Code's automatic stay.[8] Second, the contracting party can net the contract despite the automatic stay. Third, pre-bankruptcy set-offs by the contracting party or payments by the bankrupt entity cannot be avoided by the trustee unless the transfers were made with actual intent to hinder, delay or defraud the creditors of the bankrupt entity.[9] Fourth, the trustee cannot recover transfers that were made by the bankrupt entity even if the transfer was intentionally fraudulent so long as the contracting party received the transfers in good faith.[10] A major caveat

---

[6] See 11 USC § 553.

[7] 11 USC § 548(a).

[8] See 11 USC §§ 555, 556, 559, 560. One caveat, however, is that stockbrokers that are members of the Securities Investors Protection Corporation ("SIPC") are liquidated under the Securities Investors Protection Act. In those proceedings, the general provisions of the Bankruptcy Code continue to apply. See In re Government Securities Corp. v. Camp, 972 F.2d 328 (11th Cir. 1992), cert. denied, 113 S.Ct. 1366 (1993). As a consequence, Bankruptcy Code sections 555 and 559 specify that the right to terminate and net a securities contract and repurchase agreement, respectively, does not control over a contrary order by SIPA.

[9] See 11 USC §§ 362(b)(6), 362(b)(7), and 362(b)(17).

[10] See 11 USC §§ 546(e), 546(f), and 546(g).

is that these rights are available for these contracts only if the *party* meets specific criteria, commonly referred to as the "counterparty limitations."

Critical to the availability of these special rights is whether a particular contract fits within the Bankruptcy Code definitions of repurchase agreements, securities contracts, commodity contracts, swap agreements or forward contracts. The Bankruptcy Code carefully identifies the sorts of financial contracts entitled to its special protections in one of two ways. First, the Bankruptcy Code's definitions may include terms to narrow an otherwise broad descriptive definition. For example, the definition of repurchase agreement includes broad language, but limits the term of any protected agreement to one year or less.[11] The definition of swap agreement is somewhat different. It consists simply of a listing of common types of swaps and the legislative history of this definition indicates that the definition is expected to evolve over time as the market evolves. Second, as noted above, the special rights for these contracts are limited to particular counterparties. While the terms "repo participant" and "swap participant" include virtually any counterparty to a repurchase agreement or swap agreement, the counterparties entitled to the benefit of immediate close-out netting for securities contracts, commodity contracts, and forward contracts are far more limited.[12] As a result, the Bankruptcy Code provides important rights to counterparties to repurchase agreements, securities contracts, commodity contracts, swap agreements, and forward contracts. Those rights, however, are limited by the definitions of the covered agreements and by the restrictions on the counterparties who can avail themselves of those rights.

3. Practical Application of the Bankruptcy Code to a Hedge Fund Failure

While the Bankruptcy Code, the FDI Act and FDICIA offer strong statutory support for the netting of derivatives, the insolvency of a large foreign hedge fund involved in international markets would still have required resolution of some unique legal issues. A description of the likely sequence of events should such a failure occur illustrates these concerns.

To begin with, any bankruptcy of a hedge fund or other market participant likely will be preceded by a period of increasing losses and deteriorating financial condition. During this period, the counterparties to financial contracts will, as they did with the LTCM Fund, seek to closely monitor the financial condition of the fund, enforce stricter credit limits, and carefully enforce mark-to-market valuations and collateral pledges. If the financial condition of a hedge fund continued to deteriorate, counterparties might seek to employ contractual rights to terminate the contracts and set-off their obligations. This pre-bankruptcy set-off of obligations by counterparties entitled to set-off rights under the Bankruptcy Code could not be challenged by a U.S. bankruptcy trustee in a subsequent bankruptcy so long as the contracts qualified as

---

[11] See 11 USC § 101(47).

[12] Netting still may be available for these contracts, however, if the *debtor* qualified as one of the defined parties. See 11 USC §§ 555, 556.

repurchase agreements, securities contracts, commodity contracts, swap agreements, and forward contracts.[13]

Normally, in a U.S. bankruptcy proceeding involving a U.S. entity, to the extent that financial contracts can be terminated and netted, the debtor's counterparties will liquidate collateral pledged by the hedge fund in order to recover on the claims against those contracts. If there is inadequate collateral or no collateral to cover the counterparty's claim against the insolvent fund, then the counterparty must file an unsecured claim against the bankruptcy estate and, ultimately, receive a pro rata distribution. This sequence of events normally allows the direct counterparties of the debtor to limit their losses thereby reducing the likelihood that the defaults by a fund will create any "domino" effect upon the financial markets. The "special rights" under the Bankruptcy Code allow financial market participants to avoid the delays inherent in the bankruptcy process and reduce the losses that otherwise could result from any degradation of collateral pledged by their insolvent counterparty. Consequently, the right to terminate and net certain financial contracts despite a bankruptcy helps prevent the destabilization of additional financial market participants by facilitating the liquidity necessary to settle other obligations and by reducing the likelihood of a series of defaults that could undermine the overall operation of the financial markets. In the unusual situation, however, where a hedge fund has substantial positions in a particularly illiquid security or type of security, conditions in such markets could be adversely affected if many of the fund's counterparties simultaneously sought to terminate and net their exposures. These disruptions would result from creditors' attempts to realize upon their illiquid collateral, from the resulting impact on market prices and from market participants' subsequent reevaluation of their remaining exposures.

In the case of the LTCM Fund, the liquidation of foreign securities underlying certain of the Fund's repo and securities lending transactions could have been substantially disruptive. In addition, market disruption could have been caused by LTCM's counterparties' rush to replace derivatives positions they had terminated with LTCM.

The financial imperative to reduce market risk and potential future exposure will compel the insolvent fund's counterparties to terminate immediately their financial contracts and net their resulting exposures. Unfortunately, the Bankruptcy Code has no mechanism for consideration of the potential system-wide impact of an insolvency by the bankruptcy court, the trustee, or a third party. In the absence of any process for determining that the normal Bankruptcy Code obligations should give way in the interest of the broader economy, action to prevent or moderate the impact of a default must take place *before* insolvency. Once a non-bank is placed into bankruptcy, the interests of its creditors, not the markets or the economy, prevail under the Bankruptcy Code.

---

[13] See 11 USC §§ 553(b)(1) (referencing the contracts listed in 362(b)(6), 362(b)(7), and 362(b)(17)). Although Section 553(b)(1) continues to cite Section 362(b)(14), the appropriate reference should be to Section 362(b)(17), which was renumbered after enactment of Section 553(b)(1).

Indeed, the opportunity for consideration of other issues in bankruptcy proceedings is limited because the goals of the Bankruptcy Code focus on the reorganization of the insolvent entity and the payment of creditors. The Bankruptcy Code generally does not authorize third parties, such as government agencies that are not creditors of the bankrupt entity, to participate in the bankruptcy proceedings. Sections 1109(a) and 901 do permit the Securities and Exchange Commission to appear and be heard in Chapter 11 reorganization and Chapter 9 municipal bankruptcy cases. Section 762 likewise permits the Commodity Futures Trading Commission to appear and be heard in commodity broker liquidation proceedings. These provisions, however, do not provide these agencies with any decision-making power.

International issues

The resolution of a large market participant's international trading activities would create additional difficult practical and legal issues. Most international financial contracts incorporate netting rights. These contract provisions are frequently based on standard documentation prepared by the International Swaps and Derivatives Association ("ISDA"). While the laws of many nations recognize the enforceability of netting, the insolvency treatment of such contractual provisions is not assured.[14] ISDA documentation offers choice of law provisions focused on New York law and English law. The enforceability of close-out netting in insolvency proceedings is clear in both jurisdictions. Likewise, the close-out and netting provisions of a standard ISDA master netting agreement would most likely have been enforceable against the Fund under Cayman Islands law. Therefore, assuming a U.S. creditor and the Fund had duly entered into one of these agreements, the U.S. or Cayman Islands court handling the LTCM Fund's bankruptcy petition would most likely have recognized the U.S. creditor's right to exercise its contractual right to terminate any underlying swap transactions and then calculate a net amount owed by the Fund. Consequently, counterparties of a large, internationally active hedge fund could be expected to assert their rights to terminate and net their exposures for transactions documented under standard ISDA documentation.

Issues raised by Section 304 of the Bankruptcy Code

The Code's Treatment of Financial Contracts in a Section 304 Proceeding. In the specific case of the LTCM Fund, additional legal uncertainly existed because the Fund was a foreign limited partnership and was thus likely to have been wound up pursuant to a foreign bankruptcy regime. Unfortunately, in the event of a ancillary U.S. bankruptcy proceeding involving the LTCM Fund, some legal uncertainty existed regarding whether the right

---

[14] See Bank for International Settlements, "OTC Derivatives: Settlement Procedures and Counterparty Risk Management" at 14 (Sept. 1998).

counterparties to financial contracts have under the Bankruptcy Code to promptly liquidate collateral might have been undermined.[15]

While Section 304 of the Bankruptcy Code gives creditors broad rights to seek recourse in U.S. courts against any debtor with assets located in this country, the Bankruptcy Code authorizes the immediate suspension of a proceeding involving a foreign entity if the court finds that such an action is consistent with six factors, including: (i) that U.S. claimants would not be prejudiced by such a stay and (ii) distribution of the proceeds of the debtor's estate would occur through the foreign proceeding substantially in accordance with that of the Bankruptcy Code.[16] Section 304 of the Bankruptcy Code authorizes the duly selected trustee or other representative of an estate in a foreign insolvency proceeding ("Foreign Representative") to commence an ancillary proceeding[17] ("Section 304 Proceeding") protecting the assets of the foreign debtor's estate located in the U.S.[18] Once a Section 304 Proceeding has been initiated, U.S. bankruptcy courts have broad discretion in determining the type of relief to be granted a Foreign Representative. U.S. bankruptcy courts can enjoin any action against the foreign debtor with respect to its U.S. property and compel the turning over of property of the foreign debtor's estate (or the proceeds thereof) to such Foreign Representative.[19]

---

[15] However, as explained below, legislation drafted by the President's Working Group and introduced in the 105th Congress would have amended Section 304 of the Bankruptcy Code to clarify that the provisions of the Bankruptcy Code relating to financial contracts and master netting agreements apply in a Section 304 Proceeding. See S. 1914, § 210 (105th Cong., 2nd Sess. April 2, 1998) ("Grassley Bill"); H.R. 4393 (105th Cong., 2nd Sess. Oct. 4, 1998) ("Leach Bill"). This legislation was reintroduced in the 106th Congress. See H.R. 1161 (106th Cong., 1st Sess. Mar. 17, 1999).

[16] See In re Gee, 53 B.R. 891 (Bkrtcy. N.Y. 1985) (holding that a foreign bankruptcy trustee of a Cayman Islands company was entitled to relief under Section 304 of the Bankruptcy Code).

[17] Section 304 is designed to afford bankrupt foreign debtors the opportunity to "prevent the piecemeal, distribution of [their] assets [located] in this country…" by local creditors. Victrix Steamship Co. S.A. v. Salen Dry Cargo A.B., F2d 709, 713-14 (2d Cir. 1987). A Section 304 Proceeding is not a full-scale bankruptcy case. It does not offer the foreign representative either the protections of an automatic stay or the right to invoke the Bankruptcy Code's avoidance powers. In re Koreag, 103 B.R. 705, 709 (S.D.N.Y. 1991).

[18] In order to invoke a U.S. bankruptcy court's jurisdiction under Section 304, a Foreign Representative merely has to allege that: (i) a foreign proceeding was commenced against the debtor; (ii) the petitioner is a Foreign Representative and thus entitled to file the action under Section 304; and (iii) "the debtor had certain assets within the judicial district where the petition was filed." In re Koreag, 130 B.R. at 711 (quoting In re Trakman, 33 B.R. at 783).

[19] 11 USC §304(b). In a Section 304 Proceeding, temporary injunctive relief is within the discretion of the bankruptcy court and is available to Foreign Representatives on an ex parte basis for a short period of time (e.g., one to three days). Of course, losses by U.S. creditors of the LTCM Fund would arguably have been substantially exacerbated if these creditors had to wait even two or three days to liquidate their collateral following a bankruptcy filing by the Fund in the Cayman Islands.

Implications of a potential bankruptcy filing by LTCM in the Cayman Islands.
With respect to the LTCM Fund, it was quite possible that the Fund would have initially filed for bankruptcy protection in the Cayman Islands. In fact, with respect to the recent failure of the High Risk Opportunities Hub Fund ("HRO"), a $450 million Cayman Islands hedge fund that had substantial U.S. creditors, no U.S. bankruptcy proceeding occurred despite the fact that the debtor's principal place of business was Florida. In that case, HRO filed for liquidation in the Cayman Islands in early September soon after its creditors had sought recourse against the fund in the Cayman Islands court system.[20]

Operation of Section 304 of the Bankruptcy Code. U.S. bankruptcy courts have historically been quite willing to defer to a foreign insolvency proceeding involving a foreign debtor absent a substantial showing by U.S. creditors that they will face discriminatory treatment in the foreign proceeding.[21] In fact, Cayman trustees have previously had success obtaining stays against U.S. creditors through the filing of a Section 304 petition.[22]

It therefore seems possible that any Section 304 petition filed by the Cayman trustee of the LTCM Fund shortly after it filed for bankruptcy may very well have succeeded in forcing certain U.S. secured creditors to seek the permission of a foreign bankruptcy court in order to liquidate their collateral.[23] At a minimum, it may have delayed U.S. creditors from liquidating any U.S. Treasury securities pledged by the Fund under a master netting agreement.[24] The reason is that it

---

[20] Financial Times, p. 34, Sept. 3, 1998. Wall. St. J. C22, Column 3, Sept. 8, 1998.

[21] Thus in holding that creditors of a Swedish debtor "may be required to assert their claims against a foreign bankrupt before a duly convened foreign tribunal," the Second Circuit Court of Appeals sought to stress in Cunard Steamship that "American courts have consistently recognized the interest of foreign courts in liquidating . . . the affairs of their own domestic business entities." Cunard Steamship Company Limited v. Salen Reefer Services AB, 773 F.2d 452, 458-59 (2d Cir. September 19, 1985).

[22] See In re Gee, 53 B.R. 891 (Bkrtcy. N.Y. 1985). In 1985, the U.S. Bankruptcy Court for the Southern District of New York granted a request by a Cayman Islands liquidator for a stay pursuant to Section 304. In ruling for the Cayman representative, the court evaluated many of the factors specified in Section 304(c) before finding in favor of the petitioner on the grounds that Cayman bankruptcy law was not repugnant to U.S. laws and policies. In its decision, the U.S. Bankruptcy Court for the Southern District of New York found that the Cayman Islands Companies Law is quite similar to both the British Companies Act and the Bankruptcy Code, and the court was swayed by the fact that Cayman bankruptcy law did not appear to prejudice U.S. claimants or create unjust treatment of the estate's creditors.

[23] Petitions filed under Section 304 are frequently accompanied by a request for an immediate temporary restraining order ("TRO") which remains in force until a hearing on the request for an injunction can be scheduled. At the subsequent hearing, the bankruptcy court will determine whether a more permanent injunction will be granted to the Foreign Representative.

[24] With respect to HRO, it is our understanding that a U.S. ancillary proceeding under Section 304 of the Bankruptcy Code has not been initiated by HRO's Cayman trustee because creditors voluntarily agreed to the

is unclear under the Bankruptcy Code whether a stay issued in a Section 304 proceeding can temporarily prohibit the liquidation of collateral pledged to secure obligations under certain financial contracts. Although Section 362 of the Bankruptcy Code includes a broad exception to its automatic stay that expressly allows for the exercise of setoff and liquidation rights by repo and swap participants, Section 362 and its protections are not applicable in an ancillary proceeding. Therefore, it is currently not altogether clear whether a temporary restraining order ("TRO") or other stay issued in a Section 304 proceeding can prevent the exercise of these same creditor rights. Assuming a U.S. bankruptcy court granted a Foreign Representative the requested suspension order pursuant to Section 304, one of the immediate consequences would have been that U.S. creditors might have been barred from liquidating their U.S. collateral. However, the amendments to the Bankruptcy Code proposed by the Working Group on March 16, 1998, would also have helped to clarify that U.S. creditors could indeed immediately liquidate any collateral pledged to them pursuant to a master netting agreement regardless of whether a Section 304 order was issued by a U.S. bankruptcy court.

While the Bankruptcy Code does not currently address the extraterritorial reach of U.S. insolvency proceedings, H.R. 833 would clarify the circumstances under which U.S. Bankruptcy Court should coordinate with foreign proceedings. Currently, there are few international agreements governing how a foreign court or government will respond to a U.S. insolvency proceeding. Some provisions of the U.S. Bankruptcy Code do have potential extraterritorial effect. Section 541, for example, defines the property of the bankruptcy estate subject to the Bankruptcy Code as including property "wherever located and by whomever held." Similarly, 28 USC § 1334(d) grants a U.S. district court in which a case under the Bankruptcy Code is pending "exclusive jurisdiction" over the estate "wherever located." Based on these provisions, federal courts have held that the Bankruptcy Code applies to actions affecting property abroad.[25] This potentially broad international application of the Bankruptcy Code is limited by constitutional and practical considerations. Under U.S. law, jurisdiction over an individual exists only if the individual has some "presence" in the United States sufficient to confer personal jurisdiction. If there is no U.S. jurisdiction, then an entity or individual controlling assets of the insolvent hedge fund, either as collateral or by a claim against the hedge fund, is not subject to the U.S. Bankruptcy Code.[26] Resolution of the potential conflicts in the liquidation of the assets of the

---

marshaling of the fund's remaining assets in the Cayman Islands.

[25] See *e.g.*, In re Deak & Co., 63 B.R. 422, 425-28 (Bankr. S.D.N.Y. 1986) (finding that the U.S. court could assert jurisdiction over stock held outside the U.S. under 28 USC § 1334(d) and 11 USC § 541); but see Arabian American Oil Co., 499 U.S. 244 (1991) (federal statute will not be applied extraterritorially unless the statutory language reflects the "affirmative intention of the Congress clearly expressed to do so").

[26] See Fotochrome, Inc. v. Copal Co., 517 F.2d 512, 516 (2d Cir. 1975) (noting that the "automatic stay" under the Bankruptcy Code cannot be effective without "in personam jurisdiction over the creditor"); see also Bankr. Rule 7004(e) (service of process in a foreign country is permitted only if jurisdiction over the property or person exists). The cases cited in the prior footnote all involved creditors or defendants with a U.S. presence sufficient to provide personal jurisdiction in the cases.

hedge fund between U.S. bankruptcy proceedings and foreign proceedings on those assets would be dependent on cooperation between the U.S. bankruptcy court and foreign authorities. While cross-border insolvencies have been characterized by growing cooperation, reliance on case-by-case judicial approach can create unpredictability – particularly in emergency situations.[27]

Other nations also have begun to adopt laws, like Bankruptcy Code Section 304, designed to facilitate cooperation in international bankruptcy proceedings. The United Kingdom has adopted a law providing for close cooperation by its courts with countries designated by the government as cooperative in insolvency matters. Australia and the European Union also have adopted new laws to facilitate cooperation in international insolvencies. During May 1997, the United Nations Commission on International Trade Law ("UNCITRAL") approved a model act incorporating provisions recognizing a "main" insolvency proceeding to govern the resolution of the international affairs of a debtor and "non-main" proceedings in the courts of other nations to facilitate the marshaling of assets. These provisions, which were incorporated as Title IX of H.R. 833, would have helped clarify the applicability of the Bankruptcy Code especially in a situation — such as one involving the LTCM Fund — where the debtor was organized abroad but whose "center of main interests" was domestic and whose assets and principal creditors were in large part located in the U.S.

---

[27] See Harold S. Burman, "Harmonization of International Bankruptcy Law: A United States Perspective", 64 Fordham L. Rev. 2543 (1996); see also In re McLean Industries, Inc., 74 B.R. 589, 591-601 (Bankr. S.D.N.Y. 1987) (discussing complications arising from efforts to resolve claims to assets held in foreign jurisdictions); Felixtowe Dock & Ry. Co. v. U.S. Lines, Inc., 2 Lloyd's Rep. 76, 95 (1987) (English court's injunction barred removal from the United Kingdom of assets of a U.S. company in bankruptcy proceedings in New York that were claimed by U.K. company).

APPENDIX F

VOLUNTARY INDUSTRY INITIATIVES

1. The Derivatives Policy Group Initiative

The Derivatives Policy Group ("DPG") was formed by six major Wall Street firms in August 1994, to respond to the public policy issues raised by the OTC derivatives activities[1] of unregulated affiliates of SEC-registered broker-dealers and CFTC-registered futures commission merchants ("FCM"). The DPG is a voluntary framework designed to provide the SEC and the CFTC with information and analyses that would permit them to more systematically and rigorously evaluate the risks associated with OTC derivative products.

The voluntary framework applies to affiliates of registered broker-dealers and FCMs that: (1) are not subject to supervisory oversight with regard to capital; (2) primarily serve as OTC derivatives dealers; and (3) conduct OTC derivatives activities that are likely to have a material impact on their registered broker-dealer affiliates or FCMs. The voluntary oversight framework for members consists of four interrelated components: management controls, enhanced reporting, evaluation of risk in relation to capital, and counterparty relationships.

Management controls

The DPG identified two elements critical to effective management controls: (1) the integrity of the process for measuring, monitoring, and managing risk; and (2) guidelines that clearly establish accountability, at the appropriate levels of the firm, for defining the permitted scope of activities and the acceptable level of risk.

To maintain effective management controls, each OTC derivatives affiliate's board or governing body adopted written guidelines addressing:

- the scope of permitted OTC derivatives activity;
- acceptable levels of credit and market risk; and
- the structure and appropriate independence of the risk monitoring and risk management processes and related organizational checks and balances.

Under the DPG, senior management of participating firms permit business units to assume risks within approved guidelines and establish independent measuring and monitoring processes to manage risk within those guidelines. The firms must also have an independent external means of verification to confirm that adopted policies and procedures have been implemented.

Enhanced reporting

As part of their enhanced reporting obligations under the DPG framework, affiliates are required to submit periodic reports to the SEC and the CFTC covering credit risk exposures

---

[1] For purposes of the DPG framework, OTC derivative products are defined to include interest rate, currency, equity, and commodity swaps; OTC options (including caps, floors, and collars); and currency forwards.

arising from their OTC derivatives activities. The reported information focuses on credit concentration and portfolio credit quality. Credit concentration is reported by separately identifying the top 20 net exposures on a counterparty-by-counterparty basis; this requirement allows regulators to assess the credit risk an affiliate has vis-à-vis a particular counterparty. The credit quality of the portfolio is reported by aggregating, by counterparty, gross and net replacement value and net exposure, organized by credit rating category, industry, and geographic location. Affiliates are also required to report net revenue data for various derivative product lines or business units.

In addition to the periodic reporting of credit risk exposure information, affiliates are required to submit financial statements prepared on a consolidated and consolidating basis. Affiliates provide this information quarterly and include balance sheets and income statements.

Evaluation of risk in relation to capital

As part of their risk evaluation activities, affiliates must develop methods to estimate market and credit risk exposures arising from their OTC derivatives activities and evaluate those risks in relation to capital. Under the preferred methodology for estimating risk in relation to capital, affiliates use quantitative models to calculate changes in portfolio values.

To ensure that the various proprietary models used by affiliates are rigorous, the DPG developed minimum standards and audit and verification criteria that all models must satisfy before they may be used to estimate capital at risk. Standardizing risk evaluation also required a common approach to estimating potential exposure or risk of loss associated with a given portfolio of derivative products. The DPG adopted as a reasonable estimate of capital at risk the maximum loss expected to be incurred by a given portfolio of OTC derivative products once in every 100 bi-weekly intervals (*i.e.*, a probability of one percent over a two-week period). In doing so, however, the DPG also acknowledged the limitations in using this approach as a predictive tool.[2]

With respect to credit risk, firms calculate the capital at risk as equal to the net replacement cost by counterparty multiplied by the applicable default ratio published by the rating agencies.[3] For each counterparty, the affiliate estimates the potential risk of loss or capital at risk

---

[2] The DPG noted the following limitations of its capital at risk estimate model: (1) the past is an imperfect guide to the future; (2) the potential for loss beyond the estimated risk of loss remains, and the low probability events prompt the greatest concern because they are more likely to have systemic implications; and (3) capital levels that merely match estimates of capital at risk would be expected to be exhausted within the given test period.

[3] Default ratios are historically based and take into account the average maturity of relevant contracts and the credit rating of the counterparty.

on the basis of the one percent/two week standard, with the derived amount serving as a proxy for potential credit risk.[4] The derived amount is multiplied by the appropriate default ratio.

The DPG stated that these computations of market and credit risk exposures are not by themselves capital standards. Instead, affiliates need to make independent judgments about risk in the context of the entire DPG framework.

Counterparty relationships

The DPG framework also provided guidelines for relationships between professional intermediaries and their nonprofessional counterparties regarding OTC derivatives transactions. The DPG framework includes standards of behavior that are intended to discourage overreaching by OTC derivatives dealers and facilitate understanding of transactions by nonprofessional counterparties through full disclosure.

Under the DPG framework, affiliates are required to prepare marketing materials, transaction proposals, scenario or sensitivity analyses, and transaction valuations in good faith so as not to mislead counterparties. When dealing with new nonprofessional counterparties, affiliates are required to provide written statements identifying the principal risks associated with OTC derivatives activities and clarifying the nature of the relationship between the parties. Affiliates are also required to use written agreements, transaction confirmations, term sheets, or other written materials to clarify the terms and conditions of transactions. If by custom or practice no written agreements are prepared, affiliates are advised to exercise care to ensure a common understanding of the material economic terms of the transaction.

2. The Counterparty Risk Management Policy Group Initiative

In January 1999, a group of twelve major, internationally active investment and commercial banks formed the Counterparty Risk Management Policy Group ("Policy Group"). The Policy Group has said that it intends to develop better standards for risk management practices at securities firms and banks in providing credit-based services to major counterparties such as hedge funds. The Policy Group also says it will attempt to improve reporting of appropriate information to regulators and supervisors. Although hedge fund related difficulties helped precipitate the formation of the Policy Group, the scope of the Policy Group's work is broadly defined and is not limited to hedge fund relationships.

---

[4] In general, capital at risk is an estimate of the maximum potential loss expected over a fixed time period at a certain probability level. For example, a firm may use a capital at risk model with a ten-day (two business weeks) holding period and a 99 percentile criteria to calculate that its $100 million portfolio has a potential loss of $150,000. Stated differently, the firm's capital at risk model has forecasted (with a 99 percent confidence level) that $150,000 is the most the firm can expect to lose with this portfolio during the ten-day period. There is a one percent chance that the maximum loss over the period will exceed $150,000.

The Policy Group established three working groups to address issues relating to risk management, reporting, and risk reduction through shared efforts. Each working group is co-chaired by two members of the Policy Group and is comprised of other Policy Group members and market participants not part of the Policy Group (*e.g.*, hedge funds and pension funds).

The Credit and Market Risk Management working group plans to recommend best practices relating to counterparty credit and market risk management. This group will consider: (a) improving the understanding of how leverage, liquidity, and concentration issues interrelate and their implications for credit terms, collateral arrangements, and improvements in margin practices; and (b) enhancing valuation, exposure/risk measurement, stress testing, limit setting, and internal checks and balances. The group also will review issues relating to client due diligence, credit documentation, risk modeling and estimation tools, liquidity evaluation, and the role of independent controllers and auditors in model evaluation.

The Credit and Market Risk Reporting working group plans to consider the most effective ways to exchange information between major counterparties and their creditors, taking into account confidentiality concerns, and will examine how to improve internal risk management reporting. The group also will consider improving the availability of information to and from regulators, including the nature and timing of the reported information, and will review risk related public disclosure practices.

The Shared Industry Initiatives working group plans to assess how shared efforts among industry representatives might promote more orderly and disciplined management of counterparty credit risk. This group will explore potential measures such as: improved standard documentation practices, improved standard close-out and netting provisions, alternative approaches to dispute resolution among parties, opportunities for expanding the scope and effectiveness of netting arrangements, and shared initiatives for improving information on credit concentrations, valuations, and market liquidity (*e.g.*, a counterparty credit information clearing house).

The Policy Group and its three working groups have developed project plans and their work is underway. The Policy Group says it expects to publish its findings soon.

3. International Centralized Credit Database

One proposal that emerged in the aftermath of the LTCM episode, and one that the Policy Group plans to consider, is an international centralized credit database. As generally conceived, such a database would contain information about the outstanding credit exposure of hedge funds that would be reported on a timely basis by their major counterparties — banks and broker-dealers. Those creditors could access the database to learn the credit exposure of their potential counterparties. This arrangement is analogous to a mortgage lender's accessing data from a credit bureau in determining whether to extend credit for the purchase of a house. Such a database would provide up-to-date information regarding the current positions of potential counterparties in making a credit decision. To be effective and efficient, the database would need to be set up and run by the private sector, and participation by creditors and counterparties would need to be global.

Several difficult issues would need to be resolved by the private sector before a credit database could be put in place. For instance, one of the challenges posed by the creation of a database would be to find a way to meaningfully convey the risk of positions — *e.g.*, whether reported positions are collateralized and whether positions are hedged. Second, as information about hedge fund positions can change rapidly, reporting would need to be frequent to be useful. Third, it would be necessary to determine who would operate and maintain the database. The success of the database would clearly be contingent on the reliable maintenance and accurate dissemination of the information provided to it by the participants. Fourth, the question of who would be permitted to access the database would need to be addressed.

4. International Swaps and Derivatives Association 1999 Collateral Review

In March, 1999, the International Swaps and Derivatives Association ("ISDA") issued an assessment of how collateralization and collateral management programs for OTC derivatives performed during the periods of market volatility in 1997-98, including the extreme volatility associated with the LTCM episode.

The review identified lessons that collateral practitioners had learned during these periods of markets stress. The practitioners found that collateralization proved to be a highly successful credit risk mitigation tool during the market stress of 1997 and 1998. Several firms reported credit losses as a result, for example, of defaults by hedge funds in 1998 were significantly reduced or even eliminated because robust collateral agreements were in operation. However, the practitioners also emphasized that collateral does not solve all problems. It does introduce risks of its own — principally legal and operational risk, but also risks associated with the issuer of collateral assets, concentration in the pool of assets taken as collateral, correlation between an underlying exposure and collateral taken to mitigate that exposure, and the potential difficulty of selling collateral assets at a strong price. Experience over 1997-98 also indicated that problems can arise with internal data quality, the speed of market movements, and extreme conditions (such as the Russian debt moratorium and consequent disruptions in pricing transparency and market operation). Any of these potential risks can reduce the effectiveness of even the most advanced collateral management program.

Based on the lessons learned, the practitioners identified (and ISDA endorsed) 22 recommendations to enhance the effectiveness of collateral management practices.

The recommendations called for the individual institutions to review their practices and consider the applicability of measures designed to:

- understand the role of collateral in credit risk management;

- evaluate organizational structure and operational risks of the collateral management function;
- minimize collateral-related disputes;
- review policies regarding acceptable collateral types, haircuts, cash, and initial margin requirements; and
- create awareness of the legal environment in which the collateral function operates.

Other recommendations were directed to ISDA itself, which was asked to:

- establish working groups to discuss specific recommendations affecting the industry, including collateral types, haircut methodology (including the possibility of a benchmark asset pricing service), and cash collateral;
- review and enhance the structure, provisions, and negotiating mechanisms of the existing ISDA standard documents;
- continue its survey of the secured transaction laws in various jurisdictions; and
- continue its efforts to advance cross-product netting and cross-product collateralization.

Finally, several recommendations were addressed to legislators and regulators, which were urged to:

- review regulatory requirements to remove barriers to advancements in risk management methodologies and to facilitate the advancement of cross-product netting and cross-product collateralization; and
- consider simplification and modernization of laws governing secured transactions.

The review also included an action plan to promote implementation of the recommendations.

APPENDIX G

SUPERVISORY EFFORTS AND STATEMENTS POST-LTCM

1. Basle Committee on Banking Supervision

On January 28, 1999, the Basle Committee on Banking Supervision issued a report and accompanying sound practices guidance with respect to banks' interactions with highly leveraged institutions ("HLIs"), which include hedge funds. The report was issued to encourage the development of prudent approaches to the assessment, measurement, and management of exposure to HLIs.

The Basle Committee emphasizes the importance of fully understanding and prudently managing particular risks generated from banks' interactions with HLIs. The recommended sound practices include:

- establishing clear policies and practices for interacting with HLIs;
- employing sound information gathering, due diligence and credit analysis practices as they specifically relate to HLIs;
- developing more accurate measures of exposures resulting from trading and derivatives transactions;
- setting meaningful overall credit limits for dealings with HLIs;
- linking credit enhancement tools, including collateral and early termination provisions, to the specific characteristics of HLIs; and
- closely monitoring credit exposures of HLIs.

In its report, the Basle Committee emphasized that many of the risks associated with HLIs can be addressed at the counterparty level through better risk management. This additional risk management at the counterparty level is thought to have the potential of limiting or reducing the leverage of HLIs and their portfolios. While the Committee considered the direct regulation of HLIs, it determined that focusing on the bank counterparties of HLIs would be a quicker and more effective way of influencing the behavior of HLIs.

2. International Organization of Securities Commissions

The Technical Committee of the International Organization of Securities Commissions ("IOSCO") has established a Task Force on hedge funds and HLIs. This task force is studying risk management, internal controls, and disclosure issues as they relate to securities firms' interactions with HLIs. In addition, the Technical Committee and its working groups are considering ways to increase the transparency of HLI activities.

3. G-7 Finance Ministers and Central Bank Governors

The G-7 Finance Ministers and Central Bank Governors issued a statement of concerns involving HLIs and their activities in the world financial markets after its February 20, 1999, meeting.[1] They endorsed the above-noted recommendations of the Basle Committee on Banking Supervision and took note of the ongoing work of IOSCO in relation to HLIs. The G-7 will continue to review the implications arising from the operations of HLIs and of offshore financial centers, with particular attention to the possibility of additional reporting and disclosure regarding HLIs.

4. Board of Governors of the Federal Reserve System

On February 1, 1999, the Board of Governors of the Federal Reserve System issued Supervisory Letter 99-3 ("the SR Letter"), which covers counterparty risk management. The SR Letter was issued to address apparent weaknesses in the risk management systems at large complex banking organizations that may need to be reviewed and/or enhanced. The guidance expands on existing counterparty credit risk management ("CRM") supervisory materials.

The SR Letter specifically addresses four basic elements of counterparty credit risk management systems:

- the assessment of counterparty creditworthiness;
- credit risk exposure measurement;
- the use of credit enhancements and contractual covenants; and
- credit risk exposure limit setting and monitoring systems

Banks are expected to have specific policies for assessing the unique risk profiles of hedge funds, including the scope of due diligence analysis and ongoing monitoring to be conducted, the type of information required from hedge fund counterparties, and the nature of stress-testing used in assessing credit exposures to hedge funds.

The Federal Reserve guidance also notes the importance of potential future exposure in managing trading positions. Institutions must ensure that potential future exposures for both secured and unsecured positions are better incorporated into their credit analyses and limits. The need for better stress-testing and scenario analysis of credit exposures that incorporates the interaction of credit and market risks is also highlighted. The guidance points to the need for a better balance between the qualitative and quantitative elements of exposure assessment and management for all types of counterparties, not just HLIs.

5. Office of the Comptroller of the Currency

On January 25, 1999, the Office of the Comptroller of the Currency ("OCC") issued OCC Bulletin 99-2 which included new risk management guidance on derivatives and other bank activities to supplement OCC Banking Circular 277 and *The Comptroller's Handbook for*

---

[1] Member countries of the G-7, or Group of Seven, include the United States, Canada, France, Germany, Italy, Japan, and the United Kingdom

National Bank Examiners, Risk Management of Financial Derivatives. This Bulletin highlights existing weaknesses in the risk management systems within financial institutions and identifies sound risk management practices that banks should have in place for all significant derivatives and trading activities. Its perspective goes beyond hedge funds. It draws upon lessons learned, by both banks and other trading organizations, from turbulent trading conditions over the past several years. While it emphasizes credit risk, it also addresses other sources of risk, including market, liquidity, transaction, compliance and interconnection risk (*i.e.*, the risk that as market risks increase, there may be a concurrent increase in other risks).

The Bulletin provides enhanced guidance for examiners in their reviews of bank trading activities. It addresses five key risk management principles:

1. Banks must fully understand both the strengths and weaknesses of any risk management system, particularly models.

2. Risk outputs (*e.g.*, value-at-risk and pre-settlement risk) must be stress tested. Stress testing is an essential component of the market and credit risk management process, and requires the continuing attention of senior management.

3. Due diligence, careful customer selection and sound credit risk management, not competitive pressures, should drive the credit decision process.

4. Risk oversight functions must possess independence, authority, expertise and corporate stature to provide effective early warning to senior management of negative market trends.

5. Banks need to have appropriate risk control mechanisms in place for new products and markets prior to entry and on an ongoing basis.

6. New York State Banking Department

The New York State Banking Department ("NYSBD") released a report on banks' hedge fund activities on March 8, 1999, which shares concerns about these activities and emphasizes the need for changes in the regulatory examination process to address these concerns. The report identifies banks' due diligence processes and risk management practices as two primary areas in need of improvement. In addition, the NYSBD emphasizes the importance of highly developed techniques for measuring credit; less reliance on fund management reputation; and greater disclosure of financial information and risk management practices from hedge funds and other similar counterparties as a condition of doing business.

THE NYSBD report also notes deficiencies in the examination process, particularly examiners' knowledge and appreciation for new methods of credit generation. Methods specifically identified in the report are the use of leverage, out-of-the-money options trading, and off-market swap pricing.

www.ingramcontent.com/pod-product-compliance
Lightning Source LLC
Chambersburg PA
CBHW080252180526
45167CB00006B/2501